THE CHOY
OF COOKING

MUTUAL PUBLISHING

Copyright 1996
by Mutual Publishing

Additional photo credits:
Kirk Lee Aeder (Sam Choy's Kona restaurant),
Isamu Kobayashi (Sam in Japan),
Raymond Wong (Oahu farms; Sam Choy's Diamond
        Head; children eating desserts)

The trademarks Gallo, Turning Leaf, Anapamu,
Zabaco, Gallo Sonoma, Ecco Domani and Gossamer Bay
are trademarks of E.& J. Gallo Winery and are used
with permission.

Library of Congress Catalog
Card Number 96-077565

First Printing October 1996
1 2 3 4 5 6 7 8 9 casebound
1 2 3 4 5 6 7 8 9 softcover

ISBN 1-56647-128-1 (casebound)
ISBN 1-56647-135-4 (softcover)

Mutual Publishing
1127 11th Avenue, Mezzanine B
Honolulu, Hawaii 96816
Telephone (808) 732-1709
Fax (808) 734-4094
e-mail: mutual@lava.net

Printed in Taiwan

THE CHOY OF COOKING

SAM CHOY'S ISLAND CUISINE

BY SAM CHOY

Written by
Catherine Kekoa Enomoto

Book Design by
Gonzalez Design Company

Photography by
Douglas Peebles

Food Styling by
Faith Ogawa

Mahalo

It's with sincere gratitude and appreciation that we say Mahalo to each and every one of you who contributed your time, talents, energy, and Hawaiian treasures to the success of *The Choy of Cooking*. Mahalo nui loa from the bottom of our hearts!

Adaptations
Aileen Steele
Alice, Ichiro & DeeDee Yamaguchi
Aloha Airlines
Antiques & Knick-Knacks
Babs Miyano
Belinda Pali
Bentley's, Parker Square
Brian Souza
Cal Kona Produce
Chef Mike Longworth & Staff
Claire W.S. Choy
Coca-Cola Bottling Co.
Cora Buno
Craig White
Dan Akaka Jr. and Family
Dan DeLuz
Dan DeLuz's Woods, Inc.
Dave Moniz
Davo Murray
Decorative Art, Honokaa
Denise Truck
Dominique Pantohan
Donald Sasaki
Drianna Pantohan
Ed Enomoto
Ella Ignacio
Gallery of Great Things
Gary Wagner
Ginger Moon Farm
Hamakua Clay Co.

Hilda Awong
Hilton Waikoloa Village
Holly Wheeles
Hulihee Palace, Kailua-Kona
Island Herbs @ Keala'o Keawe Farm
Island Orchid Flowers
J.K. Spielman
James Key
James Lee
Jannine Cobb-Adams
Jenny Brian
Joann Ewaliko
Joe & The Boys on the Wall
Joe Rivera
John & Amy Tanaka
Jonathan Kreuger
Ka'awaloa Orchards
Kahlil Dean
Kahuku Harvest
Kamuela Price Beef
Kanani Exquisite Woods
Kanani Weller
Kari Ostman
Keali'i/T.M. Lum
Kehau Lum
Ken & Roen Hufford
Kenneth Kihe
Kona Laminates, Inc.
Kona Lobster & Shrimp Company
Kona Mushrooms
Konawaena School Woodshop,
    Guy Sasaki & Jimmy Bustu
Liberty House
Linda Bong
Locals Only
Luis D'Angelo
Lynn Lee
Marcy White
Maria Brick
Marie McDonald
Maui Hotel & Restaurant Supply
Mauna Lani Bay Hotel & Bungalows
Michelle Doo

Mike & Amy Rosato
Mountain Meadows
Nakano Farms
Nake'u Awai Designs
Nancy Teves
Neil Matsumura
North Hawaii Community Hospital
Oahu Restaurant Supply
Paniau
Paul Ah Cook
Paul Hirata
Pineapple Juice
Powers Electric
Pua Kalehua Homestead
Rick Habein
Royal Hawaiian Sea Farms
Scott Hiraishi
Scott Seymour
State of Hawaii, Department of
    Agriculture
Sun Bear Produce
Susan Tanouye-Cowan
Suzi Scott
Sweet Wind, Parker Square
The Late Felix Joyce
Tiffani Green
Tina Kendrick
Tita's Toss
TK Sales
Tom & Shirley Yamamoto
Tom Pico
Tom Steele
Tom Thomas
Toni Ann & David Souza
Triple F
Tsue Nakagawa
Vanessa Lawson
Vicki Mallion
Wai Lin Choy
Willy Pirngruber

My dad, Hung Sam Choy, is one of my idols. I can close my eyes right now and see him leaning over the sink, peeling vegetables so artistically. He lined the ingredients up in the order they'd go into the wok, or the pot, or the stir-fry — first the minced garlic and ginger, then the onion and celery, and finally the carrots and peppers for color. He'd tell me, "In cooking, it's very important to make everything uniform. Your vegetables and meats should be about the same length. When you cook, the dish becomes a complete masterpiece. Everything blends."

I remember watching Dad make chicken stir-fry. He'd arrange all the neatly cut vegetables — green beans, Chinese peas, yams, jicama, carrots, celery, onions, peppers — on a tray, wrap it up tight, and put it in the refrigerator next to the marinating chicken bowl.

Right before dinner, we kids would smell the garlic and ginger sautéing and knew it was time to come in. You could hear the crackle when Dad threw on the Hawaiian salt. First, he browned the chicken, then tossed in the onions, and then the celery. He always had his little pot of stock on hand to add juice to the mix.

The smell of fresh Chinese parsley and lily buds with five-star spice was unbelievable. It's amazing when I think about it. I'm so blessed in cooking. I grew up with a master and got to experience all of those aromas. Every time I smell these dishes, I remember my dad.

Dad learned to cook from my grandmother. They had big taro farms in Manoa Valley and Green Valley in Punalu'u, where she cooked for 30 employees. Like my dad — when she worked in the kitchen on a big job, everybody worked.

Dad was famous for his Gon Lo Mein. He made it for countless weddings, parties, and first-birthday lu'au^. Every weekend we'd chop, chop, cut, cut, clean, clean, cook, cook. My job was cleaning vegetables. I stood at the big sink washing onions, peeling carrots, celery, garlic, ginger…it seemed endless.

When my dad saw me on national television recently, he cried and cried, because he was so proud. He told me, "You know, boy, I'm happy, because you folks (sisters Claire and Moana and brother Patrick) all have grown up to be good kids…"

I'm fortunate that Mom and Dad are still around to help me, and my first dedication is to them.

Then there's the entire Choy clan — my wife, Carol Greene Choy; my two boys, Sam Jr. and Christopher; my two sisters, Claire Wai Sun Choy and Moana Wai Lin Choy; and my brother, Patrick Wing Hing Choy. Through their support, I have the opportunity to taste, talk, feel, travel, share, and educate.

I also want to recognize and thank the hard-working farmers and fishermen who devote their lives to provide the freshest and best foods.

And, finally, to all the hard-working people of Hawai'i — the folks who remember the old days and really know how to WORK. A big mahalo for being role models for our kids.

The Choy family, from left: Carol, Chris, "Hoku Aloha", myself and Sam Jr.

HEALTHY COOKING

When Sam asked that I work with him on *The Choy of Cooking* and write the foreword, I was flattered. As a member of the nutrition community, people often tell me they want healthy foods and foods that taste great. Food, as we all know, is an important part of our traditions and our celebrations. Sam should be congratulated for creating a number of recipes that meet these seemingly conflicting desires.

As one of the premier chefs in Hawai'i, Sam Choy in this book has taken that extra step to give people options in their cooking and eating styles. Nutrient information is provided for the recipes. And you will see that many of the recipes in *The Choy of Cooking* meet the strict low-fat guidelines set by the federal Nutrition Labeling and Education Act. These recipes are marked with the 🦐 symbol. When recipes in this book don't already meet low-fat guidelines, tips are provided to lower the fat without losing flavor. The good news for those who are health conscious is that *The Choy of Cooking* is about more than tasty recipes—it's about healthy cooking as well.

A unique quality of Sam's recipes is that the harmony of flavors exists without added fats and oils. Lowering the fat doesn't remove the strong, full flavor combinations of ginger and garlic, or of wonderful tropical fruits. These memorable new culinary sensations can replace old memories of high-fat foods. Moreover, less food with more flavor can be quite satisfying; so calories and fat can be managed by eating the "right" amount of food. Using fresh, high-quality, low-fat ingredients wins half the battle!

Simple, common-sense steps to "The Choy of Low-Fat Cooking" include:

• Consume all oils in moderation—even those touted as good for you. Remember cooking oils are 100% fat.

• Use a non-stick wok or skillet over a lower heat to decrease fat during frying.

• Use non-stick vegetable-oil sprays sparingly. They are almost always 100% fat although the nutrition facts panel says 0 grams of fat (a quirk of the law).

• Drain and discard cooked fat and blot fried foods to remove excess oils.

• Steam foods when possible or sauté in broths or fruit juice concentrates to carry rich flavors.

• Make sure all visible fat from meats and poultry is removed. Ask the butcher to remove visible fat, so you don't pay for it. Use the leanest cuts of meat and poultry such as beef round tip, top round, sirloin, and shank; choice leg of lamb; pork loin cuts (tenderloin, sirloin and center) and Canadian bacon; and skinless poultry—skinless chicken breast is best.

• Use nuts sparingly and where they taste best—on the top.

• Use smaller amounts of crust ingredients as toppings.

• Lower-fat substitutes include: low-fat coconut milk such as Agri-Globe and Trader Joe's brands, or blend half regular coconut milk with evaporated skim milk.

• In place of cream, use buttermilk plus a little cornstarch; buttermilk mixed with nonfat yogurt; whole milk; or half and half.

• Mix nonfat mayonnaise with a dash of horseradish or hot mustard to add zip to sandwiches and potato salad. Create a creamy low-fat dressing by using nonfat yogurt or buttermilk instead of oil.

• Substitute lower-fat whipped toppings in place of whipped cream. Use "light" cream cheese; remember to watch out for fat-free cream cheese's very different cooking and baking qualities.

• Add cocoa instead of chocolate to remove almost all of the fat of this flavoring.

• Substitute applesauce, prune purée, or jarred baby food or vegetables in the place of oils when baking breads, cakes, rolls, muffins and brownies.

Vegetarians, rejoice! You can enjoy *The Choy of Cooking* by substituting tofu, textured vegetable protein, and seitan (gluten) for meats and poultry. Freeze tofu for 24 hours to give regular tofu a ground-meat texture, or to give firm tofu a "meat-like" texture. These textures absorb the flavors of sauces well. (Please note that substituting tofu for very lean cuts of meat or poultry can increase fat and calories in a recipe.)

Finally, people with hypertension or other health conditions may want to limit their sodium intake. Please note that, per teaspoon, salt contains 2,100 milligrams of sodium; soy sauce contains 310 milligrams; "light" soy sauce contains 200; and oyster sauce contains 220 milligrams. Season accordingly.

(The Genesis R&D Nutrition Labeling and Formulation Software [ESHA Research, P.O. Box 13028, Salem OR 97309] was used to estimate the nutrient content of all recipes.)

Here's to your taste buds and a long and healthy life!

—Joannie Dobbs, Ph.D., C.N.S.

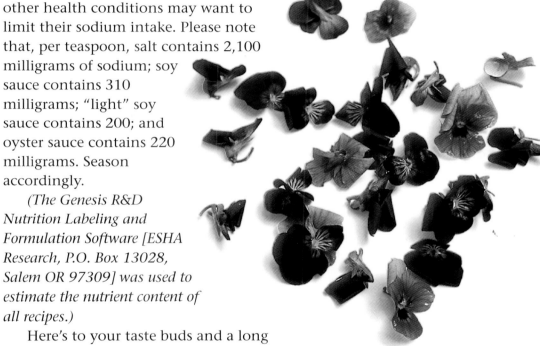

CONTENTS

x   PREFACE
xi   INNER CIRCLE OF FLAVORS

1   APPETIZERS & SOUPS
    (NA PUPU A ME NA KUPA)
3   Deep-Fried Mahimahi Macadamia
    Nut Fingers
4   Summer 'Ahi Tartare 🐾
6   Wok Barbecue Shrimp with Pepper-
    Papaya-Pineapple Chutney
7   Wings of Wings Miso
    Shoyu Chicken
8   Crab and Shrimp Stuffed Shiitake
    Mushrooms with Mango
    Béarnaise Sauce
10   Tailgate Mochi Mochi Chicken
13   Da Wife's Bean Soup
14   Kona Seafood Chowder
15   Quick and "Tastes Good"
    Barley Soup
17   'Ahi and Shrimp Candy 🐾
18   Definitely Easy Deboned Shoyu
    Chicken Drumettes
19   Best Crabmeat Soup with Taro
20   Tropical Marmalade 🐾
20   Pepper-Papaya-Pineapple Chutney 🐾
21   Mango Béarnaise Sauce
21   Fish Stock

22   SLICE (KA POKE)
25   Poke Patties
27   Straight Hawaiian-Style
    'Inamona Poke 🐾
28   Korean-Style Tako Poke 🐾
30   Aku Poke 🐾
33   'Ahi Poke Salad
34   Helena Pali Opihi Limu Poke 🐾
36   Tako Poke 🐾
37   Blue Pincers Poke

38   SALADS (NA LAU 'AI)
41   Why Not? Breadfruit, Sweet Potato
    and Taro Salad with Crabmeat
43   "Wow the Neighbors" Seafood Salad
45   Hilo Tropical Fruit Slaw 🐾
46   Lamb Salad
48   "The Old Sand Island Days"
    Ogo Pickle — "Not" 🐾
50   Nineties Style Potato Salad
51   Bella Mushroom Salad 🐾
53   Lomilomi Salmon with a Twist
54   Puna Papaya and Maui Onion
    Dressing
54   Dill Vinaigrette
55   Limu Lomilomi Relish 🐾
55   Keahole Ogo Salad with
    Miso Dressing

56   GINGER
    (KE 'AWAPUHI 'AI)
59   Ginger, Ginger Steamed Mussels
60   Ginger Clams with Black Bean
    Sauce
62   Local-Style Ginger Braised Chicken
63   Ginger Shoyu Pork
65   Spicy Braised Chicken with Ginger
66   Miso Miso Boneless Chicken Thighs
    with Ginger
69   Gingered Scallops with Colorful
    Soba Noodles 🐾
70   Braised Ginger Honey Chicken
71   Cold Chicken Tossed with Fresh
    Ginger Pesto
72   Gingered Lobster

74   WOK (KA IPUHAO PAKE)
77   Wok-Fried Lobster with Thick Soy
78   Stir-Fried Chicken with Sweet
    Peppers and Onions
80   Wok the Chicken with Eggplant
    & Hot Peppers

81   Wok Spicy Tofu
83   Sesame Ginger Snap Peas
84   Wok Pork, Pineapple Barbecue
    Sauce and Lychees
86   Garlic Shrimp with Spinach,
    Red Peppers and Oyster
    Mushrooms
88   Wok Stir-Fried Ono and Hawaiian
    Hot Peppers
89   Stir-Fried Curried Scallops 🐾
91   Pan-Fried Spicy Eggplant

92   GRILL
    (KE KAPUAHI KO'ALA)
95   Patti "O" Short Ribs
96   Yellowfin Tuna with Lime-Shoyu
    Marinade
98   Hoisin Pulehu Pork Chops
99   Tailgate Teri Steaks
101   Hilo Mango-Liliko'i-Basil Barbecue
    Shrimp 🐾
102   Backyard-Style Barbecue Ribs
104   Swordfish, Mango and Garlic
    Bread Kebabs
105   Kona Cuisine Seafood Brochettes
107   Barbecue Beef Short Ribs
108   Tailgate Anne Barbecue Leg of Lamb
109   Sweet-Bread Variations for the Grill
110   Grilled Quesadilla Variations
111   Backyard Barbecue Sauce 🐾
111   Tailgate Teri Sauce 🐾

112   LOCAL FLAVORS
    (NA 'ONO 'ONE'I)
115   Kamuela Dry-Rub Tenderloin
117   Dad's First Cooking Lesson —
    Steamed Moi with Lup
    Cheong, Green Onion
    and Ginger
118   Chicken Lu'au — My Mother's
    Favorite

119 Easter Roast Lamb
120 Easy Local Ribs
122 Christopher's Stir-Fried Chicken
123 Beef or Pork Lu'au Stew
125 Honomalino Lamb with Satay Sauce
126 North Shore Ham Hocks with Mongo Beans and Eggplant
128 Easy Holiday Pork Chop and Potato Scallop
129 Sweet Potato Casserole
131 Ka'u Mac Nut-Crusted Roast Loin of Pork with Tropical Marmalade
132 Local Boy Smoked Pork
133 Grandma's Meatloaf

134 CHICKEN (KA MOA)
137 Quick and Easy Shoyu Chicken
139 Hibachi Miso Chicken with Peanut Butter
140 Steamed Chicken with Lup Cheong
141 Kahuku Roast Chicken
142 Island-Style Barbecue Cornish Game Hens
144 Chicken and Portuguese Sausage Kebabs
146 Macadamia Nut Chicken Breast with Tropical Marmalade
147 Chicken Braised with Lily Buds and Shiitake Mushrooms
148 Stir-Fried Chicken or Beef Fajitas
150 Breast of Chicken with Shiitake Sherried Butter Sauce
151 Upcountry Sausage "Stuff It" Chicken

152 FISH (KA I'A)
155 Baked Teriyaki Mahimahi 🐒
156 Crusted Ono as Featured at Sam Choy's Restaurants

158 Lychee Oh Lychee Monchong 🐒
159 Sautéed Opakapaka with Spinach Coconut Lu'au Sauce
159 Spinach Coconut Lu'au Sauce
161 Baked Whole Opakapaka with Coconut Milk
162 Monchong with Onion Compote
164 Seared Nihoa Opah
166 Opah Macadamia Nori with Dill Cream Sauce
167 Blackened Ehu with Tropical Salsa
167 Tropical Salsa 🐒
169 Stuffed 'Ahi with Hana Butter and Papaya Coulis
170 Papaya Coulis 🐒
170 "Da Hana Butter"
171 Pan-Fried Catfish with Sam's Sweet & Sour Sauce
172 Poached Uku with Hollandaise and Poha Berry Sauce
173 Hollandaise Sauce
173 Poha Berry Sauce 🐒
174 Crispy Fish with Sam Choy's Bottled Island-Style Sweet & Sour Sauce
175 Papaya-Mango Salsa 🐒
175 Dill Cream Sauce

176 SHELLFISH (KA I'A PUPU)
179 Shrimp Curry with Coconut Milk and Sugar Snap Peas
181 Stir-Fried U-10 Shrimps and Fresh Asparagus 🐒
182 Baked Scallops Au Gratin with Fresh Asparagus
184 Cool Summer Night Cioppino 🐒
186 Braised Colossal Shrimp with Black Bean Sauce
187 Baked Coconut Shrimp 'Anaeho'omalu Bay
189 Stir-Fried Lobster and Tomatoes with Black Beans 🐒

190 Smoked Shrimp with Mango Salsa 🐒
190 Mango Salsa 🐒
191 Tomato Crab

192 SAM IN JAPAN ('AINA KEPANI)
195 Teriyaki Squid Tokyo Style
196 Ono Carpaccio with Hot Ginger Pepper Oil
198 Simmer Shoyu Sugar Butterfish with Vegetables
200 Baked Teriyaki Butterfish with Tofu
201 The All-in-One Pot Dinner — The "Nabe" 🐒

204 DESSERTS (NA MEA'AI MOMONA)
207 Hilo Haupia Squares
209 Macadamia Nut Dried-Papaya "Always Tastes Great" Bread Pudding
210 Chocolate Macadamia Cream Cheese Pie
211 Mango Bread
212 Mango Guava Sorbet 🐒
214 Three-Fruit Sherbet 🐒
214 Hibachi Pineapple Spears
216 Hibachi Bananas Foster
217 Grilled Tropical Fruits 🐒

218 WINE LIST
220 HAWAIIANA
222 GLOSSARY
224 BIOGRAPHIES
226 INDEX
SAM'S LAST WORDS

PREFACE

Hawaiian cuisine is like a summer soup. You take everything edible out of the refrigerator and cupboard, throw it into a large pot on the stove, and start adding somma this and somma that. Like the story *Stone Soup*, where everybody brought things to add to the pot.

Hawai'i's multicultural society has been putting a big variety of ethnic foods into the Island pot for decades — like the raw fish, fresh seaweed, and tropical fruits of Native Hawaiians; the star anise, fermented black beans, and steamed fish of the Chinese; the sashimi, tofu, and teriyaki of the Japanese; the sausages and sweet bread of the Portuguese.

Our cultural mix in the Islands is amazing. Because we have this unique blend of people from all over Asia and Polynesia, the traditional Hawaiian-style cuisine of *lu'au* food, plate lunches, *poke*, and *bento* has evolved to make Hawai'i a gourmet "gathering place," where talented, award-winning chefs practice their craft and the festive culinary possibilities are endless.

The Choy of Cooking, in a sense, is a somma cookbook. It offers a range of *'ono* local recipes, some gourmet creations, some low-fat and fat-free dishes, and some desserts. Since my last cookbook, *With Sam Choy — Cooking from the Heart* (Mutual Publishing, 1995), people have been asking me to find recipes for dishes they remember from grandma and grandpa. So I've included fast, straightforward Island classics like Quick and Easy Shoyu Chicken, Straight Hawaiian-Style Poke, and Da Wife's Bean Soup.

There are also some of my own favorites that I didn't have room for in the previous cookbook — signature dishes like 'Ahi Poke Salad, Best Crabmeat Soup with Taro, and Crusted Ono. All of these are featured dishes at Sam Choy's Restaurants.

For those who are health- or weight-conscious, I've included lighter, healthful, low-fat and fat-free recipes, like Summer 'Ahi Tartare, The All-in-One Pot Dinner (The Nabe), and Mango Guava Sorbet. My friend, nutritionist Joannie Dobbs, has provided nutritional analyses for all the recipes and tips on how to make each dish better for you.

My cooking keeps opening travel opportunities — to food shows, culinary exhibitions, and cooking fetes — and has taught me an international perspective. I've worked with

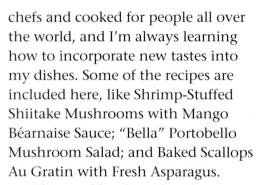

chefs and cooked for people all over the world, and I'm always learning how to incorporate new tastes into my dishes. Some of the recipes are included here, like Shrimp-Stuffed Shiitake Mushrooms with Mango Béarnaise Sauce; "Bella" Portobello Mushroom Salad; and Baked Scallops Au Gratin with Fresh Asparagus.

This cookbook is also about remembering my roots — the Chinese-Hawaiian traditions of my family, the fishermen I grew up with at La'ie beach, and all the good foods and good feelings I shared with people throughout my life at many, many get-togethers, meals, and parties.

This cookbook tries to capture the nuances of Hawai'i's famous summer soup — the savory, sumptuous broth filled with "somma da best."

I hope you enjoy it!

INNER CIRCLE OF FLAVORS

Being a good cook is simple — know your inner circle of flavors and create dishes with confidence and success. By inner circle of flavors, I mean the "inventory" of what's in your kitchen right now — the foods and spices you already know and like.

If you understand that inner circle of flavors, you can develop your own style of free-form cooking. Educate your taste buds by sampling what's in that inventory. Go through your spice rack. Open the bottles and smell the contents. Taste a bit of each on your fingertip. Then remember those spices and how you've used them in the past. You can take any recipe in this book and, based on your preferences or special dietary needs, add or omit ingredients.

You want to cook a healthful version of shoyu chicken. You understand the basic flavors. You know what tastes good to you. So remove the skin, use light soy sauce, and add fruit juices, fresh herbs, and a star anise. A winner.

What soy sauce to use? Some soy sauces are salty and may be better for marinades than for table use. Some are sweeter and lighter. There are local brands of soy sauce in regular and low-salt versions. The important thing is to find your inner circle of shoyu, to determine what sodium level you want.

Another question might be whether to substitute for cream when preparing a sauce. You may use half-and-half or whole milk. Of course, you won't get that really rich flavor, but you'll get a good idea.

I write recipes so you don't need to spend a lot of money buying new ingredients. Find things you already have on your kitchen shelves. *You can even work your way through these recipes using what you've got the first time you prepare a dish*; then the second time you can add a spice you've recently bought, and see if you like that added ingredient. Or if there's a flavor you don't find appealing, you can drop that out of the recipe.

Most chefs want you to use exactly what they use, with certain

amounts of each ingredient and all ingredients included. Maybe it's the Hawaiian way I was brought up, but that never seemed right to me. Everyone has different tastes and should feel free to mix things the way they like. That's how we do food in the Islands. So maybe these aren't recipes I'm giving you, but guidelines to make dishes that I've had success with.

Anyway, take the challenge and be creative with these recipes. But make sure you cook within your circle of flavors, because sometimes what I like might not be what you and your family like. In the restaurant business, we must be good listeners to find out what other people like, not just what we like.

In the same way we listen to our customers, you should listen to your body. I think one influence on your circle of flavors has to be what your body craves nutritionally. Some days a salad is perfect. Other times all you think about is fresh-baked bread, or a creamy dessert. Let how you feel — and what appeals to you at the moment — be part of cooking.

Have fun with these recipes.

Na Pūpū A Me Na Kupa

(Appetizers and Soups)

2

Previous pages: A lu'au on Kona's Hulihe'e Palace grounds features pupu (appetizer) and entrée specialties, counterclockwise from top left: tropical fruits, laulau (ti leaf-wrapped bundles of meat and vegetable), haupia (coconut pudding), tako poke (sliced octopus with Hawaiian condiments), 'ahi poke (yellowfin tuna with condiments), chicken long rice, pa'akai (Hawaiian sea salt), aku poke (skipjack tuna with condiments), chile water, Honomalino lamb, poi, roast pork, pa'akai, sweet potato and breadfruit, and lomilomi salmon (salted salmon salad).

In the old days, when the plantations were running full-steam, workers carried their lunches in *kaukau* tins — covered, triple-layer containers with narrow metal handles. When the midday whistle blew, everyone gathered and put all the main dishes in the middle of a circle. Each person held a bowl of rice in one hand and a pair of chopsticks in the other, and plucked the foods out of the small tin buckets. That was how the pupu (finger food) tradition got started here in Hawai'i — everyone sharing their little bits of unique cultural flavors and, I think, sometimes their dinner leftovers.

Pupus are nice for any occasion — a snack to take on a hike, or a dish for an office party, or dinner party hors d'oeuvres. All you need is a little bit of this and a little bit of

that, throw it all together on a nice platter, and the pupus are ready. Instead of cooking a whole fryer, make chicken *adobo*. If you have a little bit of raw fish, make some Hawaiian *poke* with shoyu and garlic. Put a few vegetables together with *ho'i'o* (fern shoot) and you have a salad. If you harvest some cabbage, pickle it. Appetizers set the tone for the evening. They tickle the palate and prepare people for the wonderful flavors of the coming feast.

Of course, the variety of ingredients used for pupus has changed over the years, but the concept is the same — mixing and blending a medley of dishes in a sampler presentation.

DEEP-FRIED MAHIMAHI MACADAMIA NUT FINGERS

MAKES 12 (4-PIECE) SERVINGS

3 pounds mahimahi
(dolphinfish) fillets,
cut in 2-by-3-inch pieces
1 1/2 cups minced macadamia nuts
Vegetable oil for deep-frying,
such as safflower, cottonseed
or corn oil
Tropical Marmalade

Tropical Marmalade, see page 20

Marinade:
2 or 3 eggs
1 stalk green onion, minced
1 tablespoon minced fresh ginger
1 tablespoon soy sauce
1 teaspoon sherry
1 teaspoon sugar
1 teaspoon cornstarch
Salt and white pepper to taste

This elegant pupu features all the foods that capture the essence of the Islands — mahimahi, macadamia nuts, pineapple, papaya, even cane sugar.

IN A LARGE MIXING BOWL, combine marinade ingredients and marinate mahimahi "fingers" 10 minutes; drain. Dip fish pieces in macadamia nuts to coat.

IN A FRYING PAN, heat oil on medium-high heat. Fry fish fingers a few at a time until golden. Drain briefly on paper towel and serve. Serve these nutty morsels with Tropical Marmalade.

COOKING TIP:

Roast macadamia nut bits on a dry baking sheet in a preheated 300-degree oven for 3 or 4 minutes or until lightly browned.

Approximate nutrient content per serving fish, based on
1/4 teaspoon total added salt: 290 Calories, 20 grams total
fat, 3 grams saturated fat, 120 milligrams cholesterol,
210 milligrams sodium, 3 grams carbohydrate, and
23 grams protein.

*Lower-fat tip: Eat three instead of four fingers to achieve
15 grams total fat and 210 Calories per serving.*

SUMMER 'AHI TARTARE 🦐

4

MAKES 6 SERVINGS

1 pound very fresh 'ahi (yellowfin tuna)
1/4 cup minced Maui onion
Juice of 1 lemon
2 tablespoons chopped cilantro
1 tablespoon minced fresh ginger
1 tablespoon soy sauce

1 teaspoon olive oil
1 teaspoon sesame seed oil
1 1/2 teaspoons grated fresh horseradish
1/2 teaspoon prepared stone-ground mustard
Pinch red chile pepper flakes
Salt and white pepper to taste

When you clean just-caught 'ahi, the bones always have a lot of meat. Get a big spoon, scoop it out, chop that up and make a fine poke, like tartare — the best.

CUT 'AHI into 1-inch cubes.

IN A FOOD PROCESSOR, combine all ingredients and pulsate 6 times or until of desired texture; do not purée mixture. If you don't have a processor, mince 'ahi with a knife to a uniformly coarse texture before combining with other ingredients.

SERVE WITH TOAST POINTS or crackers and shiso (beefsteak plant) leaves.

Approximate nutrient content per serving, based on
1/4 teaspoon total added salt: 105 Calories, 2.5 grams
total fat, 0.5 gram saturated fat, 35 milligrams cholesterol,
240 milligrams sodium, 2 grams carbohydrate, and
18 grams protein.

*Lower-fat tip: Serve with fat-free bread or crackers,
or with crisp cucumber slices.*

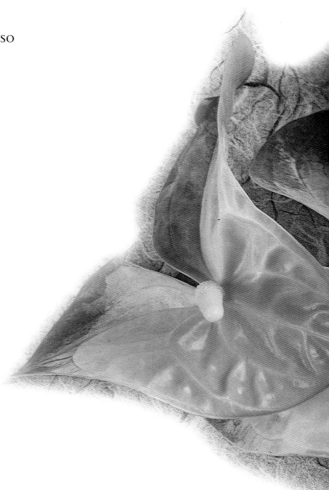

WOK BARBECUE SHRIMP WITH PEPPER-PAPAYA-PINEAPPLE CHUTNEY

6

MAKES 4 SERVINGS

Fire up wok-cooked shellfish with the zesty flavors of fresh ginger and Asian and Hawaiian chiles.

**1 pound extra-large shrimp
   (about 16 to 20)**
1 1/2 tablespoons canola oil

Marinade:
   1/4 cup canola oil
   2 tablespoons soy sauce
   2 tablespoons minced fresh ginger
   2 tablespoons chopped cilantro

1 tablespoon minced garlic
1/2 teaspoon sugar
*1 Hawaiian chile pepper, seeded
   and chopped (or 1/8 teaspoon red
   chile pepper flakes)*

Pepper-Papaya-Pineapple Chutney,
   see page 20

TO PREPARE SHRIMP, rinse and cut through shell along top of back, but not all the way through meat. Peel shell from shrimp, leaving shell and tail attached at tail. Devein.

COMBINE MARINADE ingredients and marinate shrimp 30 minutes. In a wok, heat the 1 1/2 tablespoons oil and sauté marinated shrimp 4 or 5 minutes. Do not overcook. Serve with Pepper-Papaya-Pineapple Chutney.

Approximate nutrient content per serving shrimp only: 245 Calories, 20 grams total fat, 1.5 grams saturated fat, 135 milligrams cholesterol, 620 milligrams sodium, 2 grams carbohydrate, and 16 grams protein.

Lower-fat tip: Use only 2 teaspoons canola oil in marinade and 2 teaspoons for frying, to achieve 5 grams total fat and 120 Calories per serving.

WINGS OF WINGS MISO SHOYU CHICKEN

MAKES 10 SERVINGS

5 pounds chicken wings

Marinade:

> *1 cup miso (fermented soybean paste),*
>   *available in Asian section of markets*
> *1 cup sugar*
> *1 cup soy sauce*
> *1 cup beer*
> *2 tablespoons minced fresh ginger*
> *1 tablespoon minced garlic*

IN A LARGE POT, place chicken wings and water to cover. Bring to a boil, reduce heat, then simmer 10 minutes or until done; drain.

COMBINE MARINADE ingredients and marinate wings. Grill until just brownish.

Approximate nutrient content per serving: 380 Calories, 20 grams total fat, 6 grams saturated fat, 95 milligrams cholesterol, at least 1,600 milligrams sodium, 22 grams carbohydrate, and 26 grams protein.

🍃 *Low-fat tip: Use 3 pounds skinless boneless chicken breast instead of chicken wings to achieve 2 grams total fat and 260 Calories per serving.*

Shoyu chicken with a twist: Miso always adds excitement because it's fermented, so it gives that little "wild" taste…

CRAB AND SHRIMP STUFFED SHIITAKE MUSHROOMS WITH BÉARNAISE SAUCE

8

MAKES 16 SERVINGS

Fresh shiitake speaks for itself: It's the best mushroom in the world. With crab and shrimp — Hello, it doesn't get any better. You can top it off with any sauce.

16 large fresh shiitake mushrooms, about 1 pound
1 cup heavy cream
1/2 cup chopped fresh spinach (or frozen chopped spinach, thawed and squeezed dry)
2 tablespoons chopped shallots
1/2 cup coconut milk
1 cup Ritz cracker crumbs

3/4 cup cooked Dungeness or other crabmeat
1/4 cup shrimp meat
1/4 teaspoon salt
1/4 teaspoon black pepper
Pinch fresh dill
3 tablespoons grated Parmesan cheese

Mango Béarnaise Sauce, see page 21

PREHEAT OVEN to 350 degrees. Remove stems from shiitake mushrooms.

IN A SAUCEPAN over medium-low heat, cook cream and spinach until reduced by half. Stir in shallots and cook 1 minute. Remove from heat and stir in coconut milk, cracker crumbs, crab, shrimp, salt, pepper and dill.

STUFF MUSHROOM CAPS with crab-shrimp mixture. Place caps in a shallow baking pan. Put 1/2 tablespoon Mango Béarnaise Sauce on each stuffed mushroom. Bake 8 to 10 minutes. Sprinkle tops with Parmesan cheese.

Approximate nutrient content per serving, based on 1/8 teaspoon salt in sauce: 135 Calories, 11 grams total fat, 7 grams saturated fat, 45 milligrams cholesterol, 170 milligrams sodium, 7 grams carbohydrate, and 3 grams protein.

Lower-fat tip: Reduce cream to 1/2 cup; use low-fat coconut milk, such as Globe or Trader Joe's (1 gram fat per tablespoon); and use 1 teaspoon béarnaise sauce per mushroom to achieve 6 grams total fat and 90 Calories per serving.

TAILGATE MOCHI MOCHI CHICKEN

10

MAKES 16 PUPU SERVINGS

Make-ahead tailgate pupu: This is a "local flavor" dish. It's so ono with rice — with crispiness outside and juiciness inside that contains all the flavors of the chicken.

5 pounds boneless chicken thighs,
    cut in large cubes
Vegetable oil for deep-frying, such as
    safflower, cottonseed or corn oil

Marinade:
    ½ cup mochiko (Japanese glutinous rice
       flour), available in Asian section of
       supermarkets and Japanese markets

½ cup cornstarch
½ cup sugar
½ cup chopped green onion
½ cup soy sauce
4 large eggs, beaten
4 cloves garlic, minced
1 teaspoon salt

COMBINE MARINADE ingredients, and marinate chicken overnight in refrigerator. Drain chicken pieces and deep-fry until done.

Approximate nutrient content per serving:
470 Calories, 33 grams total fat, 7 grams saturated fat,
170 milligrams cholesterol, 720 milligrams sodium,
15 grams carbohydrate, and 28 grams protein.

*Lower-fat tip: Remove skin from chicken to achieve
17 grams total fat and 340 Calories per serving.*

THEY LICKED THE BOWLS

Some of the most exciting times I've had during my mainland travels is when I cook local foods over there — showing how we do chicken hekka or throwing together a big pot of stew. For instance, if an event is on Friday, I usually have to go in two or three days ahead. So on one of those three days, just to have a little family life while I'm away from home, I always ask whoever is hosting the event, "Hey, why don't we go over to your house and have a barbecue?"

Or I cook a pot of something, depending on what time of the year it is. I remember one time I did Portuguese bean soup when it was 20 degrees below zero. The air outside was like crackling cold, like it had a sound of shivering in it even though there wasn't any wind. It was hard to breathe, and when you exhaled, your breath I think turned to little ice crystals and fell to the ground. I never knew it could get so cold. All I could think of was getting warm with Portuguese bean soup!

I was over at the house of Kevin Meeker (Chef/restaurateur of Philadelphia Fish & Co. in Philadelphia) when his family and their friends started saying, "What are we going to cook for dinner?" I said, "I tell you what, because it's freezing cold, I'll make a pot of soup." They said, "What kind of soup?" I said, "Portuguese bean soup." They went,

"Oh, Boston has a lot of Portuguese people." I said, "No, no, no, Hawaiian-style, Island-style."

Bean soup on the mainland is a thick pottage with beans cooked until very soft and sometimes puréed, whereas Hawaiian-style Portuguese bean soup is really stew-like with a thin, tomato-based broth, whole beans, and chunks of spicy Portuguese sausage.

So pretty soon I have the ham hocks going, boiling with a little garlic, onions, and celery. Just letting it boil. Making it real soft. I turn around, add dried beans. And they're going, "Will it be ready in two hours?" I say, "Relax, relax."

Oh, yeah, perfect. I'm all warm and toasty in their big kitchen, doing what I love. The trees outside the window are leafless and the white branches look like they're made of ice. I'm cooking away. Pretty soon we'll eat some hot, hot soup.

I throw the dried beans in the pot, let them go with the ham hocks. Take out the ham hocks, debone them all, chop them up. Boom, keep them separate. Let the soup keep on bubbling. Add the tomato paste. Just keep it moving. Check the seasoning. Add the vegetables — potatoes, celery, carrots, onions.

By this time everyone's sniffing the soup aromas and saying, "AAAHHH."

Chop the Chinese parsley, throw it

inside. Let it go. Salt and pepper, readjust the seasoning. Boom, they didn't have Portuguese sausage, but the spicy Italian sausage is great. Cut that all up, throw it in. Skim the fat, everything.

Two hours and five minutes later we're sitting down and having big cauldrons of some of the best Portuguese soup ever. Hooo, I tell you what, they licked the bowls! They were licking the spoons.

This guy, Chuck — a big guy with a high voice — went, "Sam, I don't care what anybody says, but I tell you what, I'm kicking my wife out and you're moving in."

Hey, let me tell you, it was a smash. Not only did it hit the spot, but everybody thought I was a god. It was just amazing. .

DA WIFE'S BEAN SOUP

MAKES 18 SERVINGS

2 cups dried beans
   (kidney, pinto or small red)
2 smoked ham hocks or ham shanks
3 cups chicken stock
1 cup chopped cilantro
2 cups diced potato

2 cups diced carrots
1 ½ cups diced onion
½ cup diced celery
1 Portuguese sausage (10 ounces)
2 cups tomato purée
Salt and pepper to taste

At family gatherings, it's the wife's soup or mine. My soup always has leftovers, her soup's always gone. (I think we eat more to make her feel better — just kidding!)

SOAK BEANS in water overnight. Drain.

IN A STOCKPOT, combine soaked beans, ham hocks, chicken stock, cilantro and water to cover (about 6 cups). Bring to a boil, then simmer until meat and beans are tender.

REMOVE SKIN AND BONES from ham hocks; shred meat and return to stock. Slice and fry Portuguese sausage, and blot with paper towel. Add sausage to stockpot along with potatoes, carrots, onion, celery and tomato purée. Cook until potatoes are tender. Season with salt and pepper.

GOES GREAT with fresh baked bread.

Approximate nutrient content per serving, based on
½ teaspoon total added salt: 290 Calories, 15 grams total
fat, 5 grams saturated fat, 55 milligrams cholesterol,
620 milligrams sodium, 21 grams carbohydrate, and
19 grams protein.

*Lower-fat tip: Use 2 pounds minced Canadian bacon instead
of ham hocks to achieve 9 grams total fat and 240 Calories
per serving.*

KONA SEAFOOD CHOWDER

14

MAKES 6 SERVINGS

All the fish from Kona — just poach it and put it in chowder. There's Boston chowder, Manhattan-style. But, hey, we can make good chowder in Hawai'i, too.

³/₄ pound firm white fish ('ahi, or yellowfin
    tuna; mahimahi, or dolphinfish; ono,
    or wahoo; sea bass) or smoked marlin
¹/₄ pound scallops
6 strips bacon, diced
1 onion, chopped
3 stalks celery, chopped
1 potato, peeled and diced
1 medium sweet potato, peeled and diced

2 cups fish stock
1 teaspoon salt
¹/₄ teaspoon white pepper
Pinch thyme
1 cup heavy cream
Chopped fresh parsley

Fish Stock, see page 21

CUBE FISH and cut scallops in half.

IN A HEAVY STOCKPOT, sauté bacon, onion and celery until onions are translucent. Add potatoes and fish stock. Bring to a boil, then simmer covered for 10 minutes or until potatoes are tender.

ADD SEAFOOD and seasonings to stockpot. Cover and cook 5 minutes or until fish is done. Stir in heavy cream and heat thoroughly. Sprinkle with parsley and serve. Great with hot fresh bread.

Approximate nutrient content per serving: 415 Calories,
29 grams total fat, 14 grams saturated fat, 100 milligrams
cholesterol, 800 milligrams sodium, 17 grams carbohydrate,
and 21 grams protein.

*Lower-fat tip: Drain 3 tablespoons bacon fat after frying and
use half-and-half instead of heavy cream to achieve 12 grams
fat and 270 Calories per serving.*

QUICK AND "TASTES GOOD" BARLEY SOUP

MAKES 8 SERVINGS

1 ¼ cups pearl barley, rinsed and drained
¼ cup plus 2 tablespoons olive oil
½ cup coarsely chopped onion
⅓ cup finely chopped prosciutto
    (2 ounces)
1 tablespoon coarsely chopped cilantro
1 teaspoon minced fresh rosemary or
    ½ teaspoon dried

1 medium potato, peeled and cut in
    ½-inch dice
1 large carrot, cut in ½-inch dice
1 can (14½ ounces) chicken stock
Salt and freshly ground pepper to taste
2 or 3 tablespoons freshly grated
    Parmesan cheese

If you do soup, pay attention to it. That's the secret. Every now and then, stir it, readjust the temperature, show your interest in it. It's going to nourish people.

IN A LARGE POT, place barley and add water to a point 3 inches above barley. Bring to a boil, then simmer partially covered for 1 hour.

MEANWHILE, IN A SMALL SKILLET, heat oil and sauté onion 3 minutes. Add prosciutto and cook, stirring occasionally, 2 or 3 minutes. Stir in parsley and rosemary; cook 1 minute.

ADD PROSCIUTTO MIXTURE, potato, carrot, chicken stock, salt and pepper to cooked barley; add a little water if soup is too thick. Cook on low heat, stirring occasionally, 30 minutes or until potatoes and carrots are tender. Stir in grated cheese immediately before serving.

Approximate nutrient content per serving, with ¼
teaspoon total added salt and 3 tablespoons cheese:
255 Calories, 13 grams total fat, 2.5 grams saturated fat,
5 milligrams cholesterol, 490 milligrams sodium,
30 grams carbohydrate, and 6 grams protein.

*Low-fat tip: Sauté onion in 2 teaspoons olive oil on
low heat, stirring frequently; also, decrease cheese to
2 tablespoons to achieve 3 grams total fat and
170 Calories per serving.*

'AHI AND SHRIMP CANDY

MAKES 6 SKEWERS

6 whole extra large shimp
(16 to 21 pieces per pound size)
6 blocks (3 ounces each) 'ahi
(yellowfin tuna)

Marinade:
1 1/2 cups brown sugar
1/2 cup soy sauce
3 tablespoons chopped green onion
2 tablespoons chopped fresh ginger
1/2 teaspoon sesame oil
1/8 teaspoon Chinese five-spice powder

Marinate large 'ahi cubes and shrimp in a thick sugary mixture. Then sear quickly, so the inside is raw and the outside is sweet with caramelized sugar-shoyu.

ON EACH OF 6 THIN STICKS of peeled fresh sugar cane or other skewers (bamboo, chopsticks, carrot sticks or other vegetable sticks), thread 1 shrimp and 1 'ahi chunk. Combine marinade ingredients and marinate skewered seafood. Grill until done, about 4 or 5 minutes.

Approximate nutrient content per skewer: 330 Calories, 1.5 grams total fat, 0.5 gram saturated fat, 60 milligrams cholesterol, at least 1,300 milligrams sodium, 55 grams carbohydrate, and 26 grams protein.

DEFINITELY EASY DEBONED SHOYU CHICKEN DRUMETTES

MAKES 4 SERVINGS

Deboned drumettes, from the largest section of the chicken wing, offer slender fillets that cook quickly and soak up flavors fast, especially the fragrance of star anise.

1 tablespoon canola oil
12 deboned chicken wing drumettes
½ cup chicken stock
3 tablespoons soy sauce
3 tablespoons sugar
1 tablespoon sake (Japanese rice wine)
   or sherry

2-inch piece fresh ginger, bruised
   (or 2 cloves garlic, crushed)
2 whole star anise, sold in small
   plastic bags in Asian markets
6 sprigs cilantro
Bean sprouts
   or shredded cabbage (optional)

IN A FRYING PAN, heat oil over medium-high heat and brown chicken fillets on both sides. Add chicken stock, soy sauce, sugar, sake, ginger and star anise; simmer 10 minutes. Turn chicken over and simmer 6 more minutes.

GARNISH WITH CILANTRO and, if desired, serve on a bed of bean sprouts or shredded cabbage. Eat hot or cold.

Approximate nutrient content per serving: 410 Calories, 27 grams total fat, 7 grams saturated fat, 115 milligrams cholesterol, 920 milligrams sodium, 11 grams carbohydrate, and 29 grams protein.

Lower-fat tip: To lower total fat per serving to 7 grams and Calories to 190 remove the skin from the drumettes prior to frying.

BEST CRABMEAT SOUP WITH TARO

MAKES 8 SERVINGS

¼ cup butter
2 cups diced onion
2 tablespoons flour
2 cups heavy cream
1 ½ cups chicken stock
2 cups coconut milk

3 cups fresh spinach, washed, stemmed
    and chopped (or 2 cups frozen
    chopped spinach, thawed)
1 ½ cups Dungeness or other crabmeat
1 ½ cups cooked and diced taro
Salt and white pepper to taste

Taro is really good when it's sweet and fresh, then poached and folded into crabmeat soup with coconut milk, spinach and sweet onions.

IN A LARGE POT, melt butter and sauté onion until translucent. Add flour and blend well. Add cream and chicken stock; simmer 5 minutes, stirring frequently. Stir in coconut milk, spinach, crab and taro; cook 3 minutes, stirring frequently. Season with salt and white pepper.

Approximate nutrient content per serving with ⅛ teaspoon total added salt: 460 Calories, 40 grams total fat, 28 grams saturated fat, 110 milligrams cholesterol, 400 milligrams sodium, 18 grams carbohydrate, and 9 grams protein.

Lower-fat tip: Use half-and-half instead of heavy cream, and use low-fat coconut milk, such as Globe or Trader Joe's (1 gram fat per tablespoon) to achieve 18 grams total fat and 260 Calories per serving.

20

TROPICAL MARMALADE

MAKES 1 CUP

2 cups diced fresh pineapple
3 cups diced fresh papaya
1/2 cup fresh poha berries
    (cape gooseberries)

6 tablespoons sugar or to taste
Chopped fresh mint or spearmint
1/8 teaspoon prepared horseradish
    or to taste (optional)

IN A SAUCEPAN, combine all ingredients except mint or spearmint. Bring to a boil, then simmer — stirring every 5 minutes to avoid scorching — for 1 hour or until mixture reaches jam consistency. Cool. Then, fold in "Sam Choy's twist" — the fresh mint or spearmint to taste.

Approximate nutrient content per 2-tablespoon serving:
95 Calories, no fat, no cholesterol, 10 milligrams sodium,
23 grams carbohydrate, and 1 gram protein.

PEPPER-PAPAYA-PINEAPPLE CHUTNEY

MAKES 1 1/2 CUPS

1 small fresh pineapple, peeled,
    cored and chopped
1 medium fresh papaya, seeded,
    peeled and chopped

1 tablespoon minced fresh ginger
6 tablespoons sugar
1 tablespoon hot chile paste, such as
    Southeast Asian sambal

IN A MEDIUM SAUCEPAN, combine all ingredients except chile paste. Cook on medium heat 1 hour or until mixture has a syrupy consistency. Fold in chile paste.

Approximate nutrient content per 2-tablespoon serving:
50 Calories, no fat, no cholesterol, 65 milligrams sodium,
12 grams carbohydrate, and 0.5 gram protein.

Mango Béarnaise Sauce

Makes 16 Servings

1 tablespoon canola oil
3/4 cup butter
2 shallots, peeled and finely chopped

2 or 3 sprigs fresh tarragon, chopped
2 sprigs fresh parsley, chopped
1/2 cup diced fresh mango
2/3 cup vinegar

Pepper and salt to taste
3 egg yolks at room temperature
2 tablespoons cold water

To make vinegar reduction: In a saucepan, heat oil and 1 tablespoon butter. Add shallots, half of the tarragon, half of the parsley, 1/4 cup of the mango, vinegar and pepper. Cook over gentle heat 20 minutes or until only 1 tablespoon liquid remains.

To clarify butter: In a bowl standing over a pan of hot water, melt remaining (11 tablespoons) butter. After several moments, milk solids will settle on bottom of pan. Pour off clear butter into another bowl, leaving milky residue behind.

To finish béarnaise: In a bowl standing over a pan of hot water, combine egg yolks and vinegar reduction; whisk well. Gradually incorporate cold water, salt and pepper, continuing to whisk vigorously until mixture becomes creamy. Remove bowl from heat and continue whisking, adding melted butter in a thin stream to make a very smooth sauce.

Stir remaining tarragon, parsley and mango into mixture. Use béarnaise immediately or reserve in a bowl standing over a pan of hot, but not boiling, water.

Fish Stock

Makes 6 Servings

1 onion
4 stalks celery
1 carrot
2 pounds fish bones, rinsed

1 cup white wine
1-inch piece ginger, crushed
1 1/2 teaspoons salt
1/2 teaspoon pepper

Coarsely chop onion, celery and carrot. In a large stockpot, combine all ingredients and water to cover, about 6 cups. Bring to a boil, then simmer 45 minutes. Strain and store in refrigerator until time to use.

Ka Poke
(Slice)

24

Previous pages: Christopher Choy, left, chops fresh ogo (seaweed) and Sam Choy Jr. slices 'ahi to prepare poke.

Below: First, sprinkle in chopped ogo; second, add soy sauce; third, mix the poke.

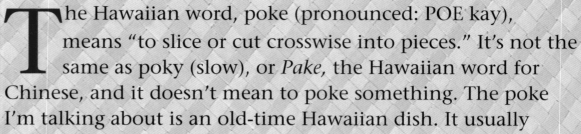

The Hawaiian word, poke (pronounced: POE kay), means "to slice or cut crosswise into pieces." It's not the same as poky (slow), or *Pake*, the Hawaiian word for Chinese, and it doesn't mean to poke something. The poke I'm talking about is an old-time Hawaiian dish. It usually consists of sliced raw fish, *limu* (seaweed), fresh red chile pepper, Hawaiian sea salt, and *'inamona* (roasted, ground, and salted *kukui* nuts).

My favorite is raw *enenue* (rudder fish) poke, because it has such a strong *limu* flavor. I add a little raw *wana* (sea urchin) and raw spiny lobster tail meat. This was a pre-Western contact delicacy. Traditional poke evolved when the immigrants to the Islands added new flavors—Japanese soy sauce, Korean kim chee, Maryland blue crab, and Nova Scotia small clams. It can be a side dish or pupu, served with rice or (my favorite) poi.

Poke has become so popular that every year we sponsor the Sam Choy/Aloha Festivals International Poke Recipe Contest. We get hundreds of entries from all over the world. Famous chefs, regular people, old fishermen prepare their favorite poke dishes for a panel of judges. We even have a celebrity competition. It's amazing to me that people from as far away as the East Coast on the mainland have poke recipes. I didn't think they liked raw fish.

I've included a variety of different poke recipes in this chapter. Come, try.

POKE PATTIES

MAKES 2 PATTIES

**Panko (packaged Japanese-style fine
bread crumbs) or Italian bread crumbs**
2 tablespoons canola oil

Patties:
    **1 cup diced very fresh 'ahi (yellowfin tuna)
        or aku (skipjack tuna), cut in about
        1/4- to 3/8-inch cubes**
    1/4 cup minced onion
    1/4 cup minced green onion
    1 egg

**2 tablespoons chopped fresh ogo
    (edible seaweed)**
2 tablespoons soy sauce
1 teaspoon sesame oil
Pinch EACH salt, pepper

Sauce:
    1/4 cup sliced mushrooms
    2 tablespoons butter
    1 teaspoon soy sauce
    1 teaspoon oyster sauce
    1 teaspoon chopped cilantro

*This is like tartare,
except we cut the fish in
tiny cubes and make a
patty similar to a ham-
burger. We sear it, yet on
the inside it's rare, with
poke-style seasoning.*

COMBINE PATTY INGREDIENTS and form 2 patties. Press patties in panko to coat.
In a frying pan, heat oil over medium-high heat. Gently place patties in pan and
brown both sides, keeping the inside of patties medium rare.

TO MAKE SAUCE, sauté mushrooms in butter 2 minutes. Add remaining sauce
ingredients and cook 1 minute. Pour sauce over patties and serve as pupu, or appetizers.

Approximate nutrient content per patty, based on 1/16
teaspoon total added salt: 490 Calories, 31 grams total fat, 9
grams saturated fat, 170 milligrams cholesterol, at least 1,500
milligrams sodium, 25 grams carbohydrate, and 26 grams
protein.

*Lower-fat tip: Use only 2 teaspoons canola oil and 1 tablespoon
butter, and substitute 2 egg whites for the egg to achieve
14 grams total fat and 340 Calories per serving.*

STRAIGHT HAWAIIAN-STYLE 'INAMONA POKE 27

MAKES 6 (1/2-CUP) SERVINGS

1 pound very fresh raw aku (skipjack tuna),
    'ahi (yellowfin tuna) or other fish,
    cut in bite-size cubes
1 small ball limu kohu (edible red seaweed
    — about 1/2 cup chopped)

'Inamona (roasted, mashed, salted
    kukui nut; see note) to taste (about
    1 teaspoon), available at island fish
    markets and Hawaiian delicatessens
1 Hawaiian red chile pepper, minced
Salt to taste

RINSE AND CHOP limu kohu. In a
mixing bowl, combine all ingredients.

NOTE: *Can substitute 1 1/2 teaspoons
cashew nuts, roasted, mashed, salted.*

Approximate nutrient content per serving, based on 1/3
teaspoon total added salt: 80 Calories, 1 gram total fat, 0.5
gram saturated fat, 35 milligrams cholesterol, at least 160
milligrams sodium, no carbohydrate, and 17 grams protein.

*Taste of old—this recipe
is simple, straightforward.
It definitely brings back
a lot of memories of my
old days picking limu
from certain parts of the
ocean and Hukilau Bay.*

*Poho kukui (kukui lamp) is a stone holder for ignited nuts
from the kukui (candlenut) tree. Kukui also provides
'inamona — a salted paste used for flavoring poke.*

TURNING LEAF.

CALIFORNIA

Chardonnay

1994

KOREAN-STYLE TAKO POKE

MAKES 6 SERVINGS

Ethnic variation: In this poke, Korean garlic-chile sauce offers a really exciting flavor; you could make your own — just grind up garlic and local peppers with salt.

2 pounds fresh ogo (edible seaweed)

1 pound tako (octopus)

1 Maui onion, diced

1/2 cup chopped green onion

1 cup rice vinegar, available in Asian section of markets

1/2 cup soy sauce

1/2 cup sugar

3 tablespoon roasted sesame seeds

2 tablespoons bottled Korean kochu jang (hot chile paste), available in Asian section of supermarkets and in Asian markets

1 teaspoon minced fresh ginger

2 cloves garlic, minced

CUT OGO in 2-inch lengths. Cook tako and slice. In a mixing bowl, combine all ingredients.

SERVE VERY COLD at tailgate and backyard barbecues.

Approximate nutrient content per 1/2 cup serving: 65 Calories, 1 gram total fat, no saturated fat, 10 milligrams cholesterol, 470 milligrams sodium, 8 grams carbohydrate, and 7 grams protein.

TURNING LEAF.

CALIFORNIA

Chardonnay

1994

AKU POKE 🦐

MAKES 8 (1/2-CUP) SERVINGS

Aku, aku: I fish a lot out there on the waters — seeing all the aku jumping all over the place, knowing there's a big marlin or 'ahi underneath trying to get him.

It's interesting to see the food chain in the ocean: The aku chases small shrimps or nehu (anchovies) or squid. Then, right below them are the big predators — yellowfin tunas and marlins. And, right below are the sharks. Everybody is just waiting their turn, up the food-chain ladder. I think it's really neat.

1 pound very fresh 'aku (skipjack tuna) or ahi (yellowfin tuna)

1 cup rinsed and chopped fresh limu (edible seaweed)

1/2 cup chopped onion

2 tablespoons soy sauce

1 teaspoon sesame oil

1 Hawaiian red chile pepper, seeded and minced (or 1/2 teaspoon red chile pepper flakes)

CUBE RAW FISH, about 1/2 to 3/4 inch square. Use fresh seaweeds, such as limu manauea (ogo), lipoa, wawae'iole or limu kohu, or a combination of them.

COMBINE ALL INGREDIENTS and mix well. Refrigerate in a covered bowl until served.

Approximate nutrient content per serving:
75 Calories, 1 gram total fat, 0.5 saturated fat,
25 milligrams cholesterol, 260 milligrams sodium,
1 gram carbohydrate, and 14 grams protein.

Sam Jr. and I fish aboard "Roxy" off the Kona coastline.

500 'AHI

Kona is my home on the west coast of the Big Island of Hawai'i. There's a lot of seafood in Kona. It's one of the most ideal fishing locations in the world because the water is flat almost all year long.

You can skewer the fresh-caught fish, throw it on the hibachi, and 20 minutes later you have a world-class dinner. Kona seafood is a great way to simplify meal preparation with good-quality food.

As a fisherman and a chef, in my lifetime I have filleted at least 500 'ahi (yellowfin tuna) ranging in size from 100 to 200-plus pounds. There's not really much challenge in cutting the tunas, once you get the hang of it. It's very quick. You cut both the smaller aku (skipjack tuna) and the larger 'ahi in the same way. You just learn to master where to cut and how hard to press. You pop the head off and go from there.

You need a little finesse. But you also need to know that you don't have to be afraid that the knife will cut too deeply into the fillet; when you hear the knife hit bone, you run the blade right along the spine of the fish and keep it straight from there.

Veterans who fillet fish use good, sharp knives. In fact, the secret of cooking is using a sharp knife with a sharp blade and a sharp tip. I like French knives with long, wide blades. These are probably the most universal and can be used for chopping, slicing, cutting, and transferring the food from counter to bowl or pan on the flat, wide blade. To fillet a large, 40-pound mahi-mahi, use a long, thin, heavier knife.

The second most important step to filleting is practice. There's a technique involved that you master over time. It's like people who first start out in typing. I'm sure they can type about 20 or 30 words a minute. Then, after a little practice, they get faster. It's the same process. When experienced fish cutters do a big 'ahi, they can "drop it off the bone" in quarters — four fillets — in less than 10 minutes.

So when I say I've filleted 500 'ahi through all those years, it's not really that much. Try doing one yourself to get the feel of cutting, and you will appreciate the taste of the fish even more.

A lot of people who start into cutting fish for their own fillets ask me how I get the fish smell off my hands. They scrub and scrub and it doesn't come out. It makes them not want to cut fish anymore. But the smell is easy to take care of. I used to have a method that I thought was the best, and when I was out in Alaska a few years ago on a herring boat one of the crewmen — and these guys handle herring fish all day —

asked me, "How do you keep your hands from smelling?" I said, "Hey, soap, water, a little lemon," and he started laughing. "I'll show you a little trick," he said. I know this might sound crazy, but it worked, and I've used the method ever since. He showed me that all you need is a little liquid soap and granulated sugar, and water to rinse. Mix the liquid soap and sugar together into a paste, rub it all over your hands and let it sit for 30 seconds or longer, then rinse. The fishy smell is absolutely gone!

Cutting fish is easier and cleaner than people think. Try it.

'AHI POKE SALAD

MAKES 2 SERVINGS

¹/₂ cup canola oil
2 (10-inch) wheat-flour tortillas
4 ounces very fresh 'ahi (yellowfin tuna),
    cut in 1-inch cubes
1 tablespoon chopped onion
1 tablespoon chopped green onion

1 tablespoon chopped fresh ogo
    (edible seaweed)
2 tablespoons soy sauce
1 teaspoon sesame oil
1 handful mixed fresh salad greens
¹/₂ cup cooked somen (Japanese thin
    white wheat noodles)

We've taken poke to new levels and developed some interesting salads. This one represents an innovation which has been very well received all over.

IN A FRYING PAN, heat oil on medium-high heat. Fry tortillas, one at a time, until golden brown; blot with paper towels to remove excess oil.

PREPARE POKE by combining 'ahi, onions, ogo, soy sauce and sesame oil; mix well.

TO ASSEMBLE SALAD, layer on a plate 1 tortilla followed by the greens, the other tortilla, somen and poke.

Approximate nutrient content per serving: 390 Calories, 16 grams total fat, 1.5 grams saturated fat, 25 milligrams cholesterol, at least 1,250 milligrams sodium, 39 grams carbohydrate, and 22 grams protein.

Lower-fat tip: Use a total of 30 low-fat tortilla chips in place of fried tortillas to achieve 7 grams total fat and 240 Calories per serving.

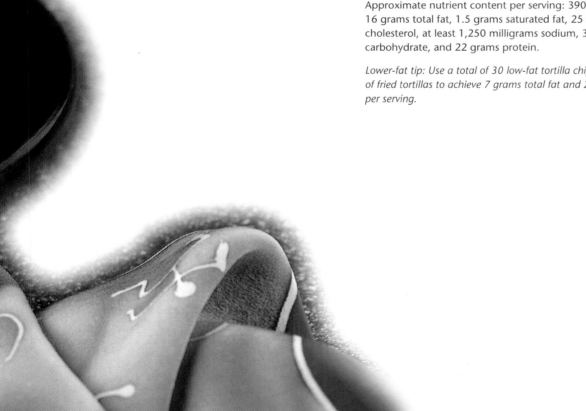

Helena Pali Opihi Limu Poke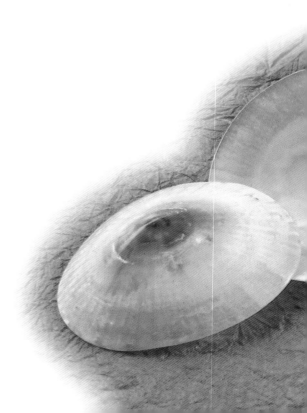

Makes 36 (1-Tablespoon) Servings

*Oregon has limpets, too,
with a hole inside.
There, they eat it raw.
It's real good, better than
our Hawaiian opihi.
In New Zealand, opihi is
like rubbish.*

**2 cups shelled fresh opihi (edible limpets
with a chewy texture similar to abalone)**

**1/2 cup chopped limu huluhuluwaena (dark
red seaweed) or other fresh seaweed**

1/8 teaspoon Hawaiian (sea) salt

SHELL THE OPIHI by scooping meat out with a spoon. Place shelled opihi in a colander, sprinkle with Hawaiian salt and rinse with cold running water. Repeat this process two or three times to remove slime.

PLACE RAW OPIHI in a bowl, and fold in limu and 1/8 teaspoon Hawaiian salt. Chill until served.

THIS DELICACY is served by the tablespoon at lu'au.

Approximate nutrient content per 1-tablespoon serving:
10 Calories, no fat, 5 milligrams cholesterol, 30 milligrams
sodium, 1 gram carbohydrate, and 1 gram protein.

TAKO POKE 🐙

MAKES 8 SERVINGS

The ancient Hawaiians made this poke with raw he'e (octopus), using the ink and everything — that's one of my favorites. You gotta chew, though...

1 pound tako (octopus)
1 ripe medium tomato, chopped
1 cup chopped cucumber
1/2 cup chopped onion

3 tablespoons soy sauce
1 teaspoon sesame oil
1 Hawaiian red chile pepper, seeded and minced (or 1/2 teaspoon red chile pepper flakes)

TO CLEAN FRESH OCTOPUS, turn head inside out and remove ink sac, innards and mouthparts; rinse. To tenderize fresh octopus, freeze, pound or lomi (massage).

TO COOK OCTOPUS, in a medium pot, bring enough water to cover octopus to a boil. Lower octopus into boiling water, return water to a rolling boil, then cook 2 or 3 minutes. Drain, plunge into cold water and slice into thin slices. In a bowl, combine all ingredients and mix well.

COOKING TIP:

To make tako soft, you can put it in a pot and pound, pound, pound. Or throw it in tenderizer. Or put it in the freezer; I freeze it.

To clean tako, turn the head inside out and take the ink bag out.

I don't like to overcook tako. Boil just enough water to cover the tako — some people use beer or sake, but I use just water. Add the tako and after the water comes back to a boil, cook it a couple minutes more. Then, rinse it in cold water real quick to stop the cooking, slice it and make the poke.

You don't want to boil and boil. Then it gets like rubber. You might as well cut up your slipper and marinate it.

Approximate nutrient content per 1/2-cup serving:
65 Calories, 1.5 grams total fat, 0.5 saturated fat, 25 milligrams cholesterol, 480 milligrams sodium, 3 grams carbohydrate, and 10 grams protein.

BLUE PINCERS POKE

MAKES 8 SERVINGS

4 pounds live blue crab
1 cup diced fresh ogo (edible seaweed)
1 cup diced onions
1/2 cup diced green onion

2 tablespoons sesame oil
1 1/2 cups Korean kim-chee base,
   homemade or prepared from a
   commercial mix
Hawaiian (sea) salt to taste

Blue pincers crab from Maryland is very tasty, very sweet. Always, you want to use live crab for poke; salt it first, let it get miko (tasty with salt). Real good.

CHILL INGREDIENTS and utensils until preparation time.

TO CLEAN CRABS, lift off back and remove gills and mouthparts. Cut body into clusters.

IN A LARGE MIXING BOWL, fold together crab, ogo, onions and sesame oil.
Add kim-chee base a little at a time to get the exact potency of chile-pepper flavor desired. Adjust seasoning with Hawaiian salt, if necessary. Meld flavors by chilling in a covered bowl until serving time.

Feathery strands of fresh ogo, or seaweed, add a crunchy taste of the ocean to salads and fish dishes.

Approximate nutrient content per 1/2-cup serving with no added salt: 110 Calories, 4 grams total fat, 0.5 gram saturated fat, 25 milligrams cholesterol, 2,550 milligrams sodium, 11 grams carbohydrate, and 11 grams protein.

Lower-fat tip: Use only 1 tablespoon sesame oil to achieve 2 grams total fat and 100 Calories per serving.

Na Lau ʻAi
(Salads)

40

After a day at the beach, or just driving around the island, one of my favorite things to do is stop at a lunch wagon or local drive-in for a plate lunch. It's like heaven to walk up to the window and smell all the different main dishes cooking—Japanese teriyaki, Korean *kal bi* (barbecue short ribs), Hawaiian *laulau* (vegetable and meat bundles), and local-style chicken long rice. All these ethnic foods are plate-lunch staples, along with the ever-constant side order of macaroni salad.

A plate lunch might feature Western-style roast pork, but in Hawai'i we prepare it differently. First, we put it over two scoops of rice, then cover it with moist pan gravy, throw on a side of salad, and there it is. *'Ono*-licious.

But it's just not a Hawaiian plate lunch without macaroni or (sometimes) potato salad. This good starch stuff adds the finishing touch. Without it, the rest of the food doesn't seem to taste as good.

To most mainlanders, salad means fresh greens, but here in Hawai'i it's macaroni salad that makes the plate lunch so special. There's an old joke—if Caucasians are coming to the dinner or *lu'au*, somebody better bring a green salad.

I put some green salad recipes in here, some with fish and chicken, Asian flavorings, and salads that can be whole meals, but I didn't forget the real stuff—the macaroni and potato.

WHY NOT? BREADFRUIT, SWEET POTATO AND TARO SALAD WITH CRABMEAT

MAKES 18 (¹/2-CUP) SERVINGS

1 breadfruit, about 4 cups chopped
2 medium sweet potatoes
1 medium taro corm, about 2 cups chopped
2 cups shredded crabmeat
4 hard-boiled eggs, chopped
¹/2 cup minced celery

¹/2 cup grated carrots
¹/2 cup minced Maui onion
1 tablespoon minced fresh dill
2 ¹/2 cups mayonnaise
Salt and pepper to taste

You bite into the taro and ask, what is this? Then you bite into the bread-fruit. Hmm, interesting and delicious. I enjoy sharing things I like.

PEEL BREADFRUIT, sweet potatoes and taro. Cut in 1-inch cubes. Cook in lightly salted boiling water until fork-tender. Cool.

IN A LARGE MIXING BOWL, toss all ingredients lightly to combine. Adjust seasoning with salt and pepper, if necessary.

COOKING TIP:
Cutting terms, in the order of increasing size, are:
• Mince
• Finely chop
• Julienne (for thin matchstick strips)
• Chop (or dice for uniform size)
• Coarsely chop
• Slice (up to 1 inch long)
• Cut into bite- (or other) size pieces or cubes

Approximate nutrient content per serving, based on 1 teaspoon total added salt: 340 Calories, 26 grams total fat, 4 grams saturated fat, 75 milligrams cholesterol, 370 milligrams sodium, 24 grams carbohydrate, and 6 grams protein.

🦀 *Low-fat tip: Substitute 2 ¹/3 cups nonfat mayonnaise mixed with 2 tablespoons regular mayonnaise to achieve 3 grams total fat and 150 Calories per serving.*

The purple sweet potato is a staple of Okinawa.

"WOW THE NEIGHBORS" SEAFOOD SALAD

MAKES 8 MAIN-DISH SERVINGS

Salad:

1/2 pound large shrimp
  (about 10 to 12), peeled and deveined
10 ounces fresh opah
  (moonfish) fillets, cubed
1/2 pound scallops
12 green mussels
1/2 pound fusille (spiraled pasta)
2 tablespoons olive oil
4 ounces smoked Pacific salmon,
  cut in 1-inch cubes
1 cup chopped fresh radicchio
1 cup fresh oyster mushrooms, cut in half
1/2 cup sliced fresh shiitake mushrooms
1/2 cup julienned red bell pepper
1/2 cup julienned yellow bell pepper

1/2 cup chopped fresh basil leaves
1/2 teaspoon salt
1/4 teaspoon black pepper
1/4 teaspoon minced fresh dill

Poaching liquid:
  3 cups water
  1 cup white wine
  1 cup diced celery
  1/2 cup diced onions, celery and carrots
  Juice of 1 large orange
  1 1/2 teaspoons salt
  1/4 teaspoon cracked pepper
  1 sprig fresh dill
  Pinch thyme

Dill Vinaigrette, *see page 54*

There's a whole abundance of things in this recipe — shrimp, the kitchen sink. You bring it to the neighbors. After they look in the bowl, they will always say, wow! It's just sharing and caring, Hawai'i style.

IN A STOCK POT, combine all poaching-liquid ingredients and bring to a boil. Add shrimp and return liquid to a boil; then remove shrimp to a plate.

RETURN POACHING LIQUID to a boil, and add opah, scallops and mussels. As soon as mussel shells open, remove pot from heat and transfer seafood to the plate with shrimp; cool.

COOK FUSILLE according to package directions, drain and toss with olive oil. In a large bowl, combine all salad ingredients and toss lightly with Dill Vinaigrette. Chill until serving time.

Approximate nutrient content per serving, based on no added salt in vinaigrette: 470 Calories, 26 grams total fat, 3.5 grams saturated fat, 85 milligrams cholesterol, 620 milligrams sodium, 32 grams carbohydrate, and 26 grams protein.

Lower-fat tip: Use only 3 tablespoons olive oil in salad — toss pasta with 1 tablespoon and add 2 tablespoons in vinaigrette — to achieve 8 grams total fat and 310 Calories per serving.

HILO TROPICAL FRUIT SLAW

MAKES 8 (1-CUP) SERVINGS

1 Puna papaya, seeded,
   peeled and thinly sliced
1 cup Lana'i pineapple,
   peeled and thinly sliced
1 medium mango,
   peeled and thinly sliced
1 star fruit, ribs trimmed,
   thinly sliced and seeded
1 kiwi fruit, peeled and thinly sliced
6 Waimea strawberries,
   hulled and quartered

½ cup whole poha berries
   (cape gooseberries)
1 Big Island banana, sliced
1 medium head radicchio, leaves separated

Hilo Tropical Fruit Slaw Dressing
   1 ripe Puna papaya, seeded and peeled
   ½ cup plain yogurt
   2 tablespoons honey
   ¼ teaspoon EACH salt, white pepper

At the Hilo Open Market you can see all the fresh fruits. So I brought out a file recipe and created a slaw using the fruits. This is ideal with broiled chicken breast.

MACHINE PROCESS dressing ingredients 30 seconds. Makes 2 cups.

IN A LARGE SALAD BOWL, combine fruits and fold in prepared dressing.
Serve on radicchio leaves.

Approximate nutrient content per serving fruit slaw:
130 Calories, 1 gram total fat, no saturated fat, no cholesterol, 85 milligrams sodium, 31 grams carbohydrate, and 2 grams protein.

Approximate nutrient content per 2-tablespoon serving dressing: 20 Calories, no fat, no cholesterol, 40 milligrams sodium, 4 grams carbohydrate, and 0.5 gram protein.

Left: The unusual-looking rambutan, lower right in photo, is an example of the exotic new fruits growing in Hawai'i. Rambutan tastes like lychee.

LAMB SALAD

46

MAKES 2 MAIN-DISH SERVINGS

You take wilted spinach salad and squirt some great dressing on it. Whew, the flavors are explosive. I mean, it's simple as that.

2 tablespoons canola oil
10 ounces lean lamb loin, cut in
    1-inch strips
2 cups fresh spinach leaves, cleaned
¼ cup chopped macadamia nuts
1 tablespoon olive oil
1 tablespoon balsamic vinegar

Marinade:
  1 tablespoon soy sauce
  1 tablespoon brown sugar
  1 tablespoon chopped fresh ginger
  1 tablespoon chopped garlic
  1 tablespoon chopped green onions
  1 tablespoon chopped cilantro
  1 teaspoon red chile pepper flakes

COMBINE MARINADE ingredients and marinate lamb.

IN A SALAD BOWL toss spinach, macadamia nuts, olive oil and vinegar. Set aside.

IN A HEAVY SKILLET, heat canola oil over medium-high heat. Cook lamb strips about 3 minutes for medium rare; longer for well done. Arrange lamb over salad and dig in.

Approximate nutrient content per serving: 530 Calories, 38 grams total fat, 6 grams saturated fat, 95 milligrams cholesterol, 600 milligrams sodium, 15 grams carbohydrate, and 33 grams protein.

Lower-fat tip: Use only 2 tablespoons macadamia nuts and 2 teaspoons olive oil in salad, and cook lamb in nonstick pan with 1 teaspoon canola oil, to achieve 20 grams total fat and 360 Calories per serving.

SUGAR PEAS, PLEASE

The growers who produce Hawai'i's vegetables and fruits are a really underestimated group of people. They have done a great job in diversifying for our needs.

I remember first talking to farmer Ben of Kohala and he asked, "How many sugar peas do you use?"

I said, "Well, I can use close to a hundred pounds a week."

He said, "Oh, only a hundred pounds? That's all?"

"Yes."

"Oh, we can grow that."

Well, halfway through the crop, I got a call. Ben said, "Ho, man, it's hard work, you know. Picking is a killer. It's never-ending. Every second they're blooming and we have to pick."

It's true, you can't let the peas grow too big because they get tough. But Ben steadily supplies the Kona restaurant with 100 pounds of tender pods each week.

Our fresh ginger all comes from Honaunau Market. Organic farmers/wholesalers Tane and Maureen Datta of Honaunau get all the local things for us — baby lettuce, salad mix, spinach, radicchio, edible flowers and culinary herbs. Harvey Sacarob of Sun Bear Produce in Honaunau organically grows all of my lettuces. We buy almost $8,000 worth of lettuces a

month from him for the Kona and Kapahulu restaurants.

We have to know what's growing at what times of year and what's not. Right now there's a shortage of poha berries, the little "lantern encased" fruits known as cape gooseberries. The shortage limits us in making fresh fruit desserts. We don't even have frozen poha berries. But when they're in stock, watch out — you've never had such an interesting taste in your dessert.

New diversified products that have appeared recently in Hawai'i include interesting things like an underground apple, similar to jicama. It's a moist, sweet, starchy item and you can eat it raw. I have to learn how to use it. It could be the new pineapple industry.

I'm hoping for more enterprising farmers to take up a lot more ogo growing, and I'd like to experiment with new ways of using it. Ogo is sea salad. In the old days the most fertile ground on O'ahu for growing ogo was out on Sand Island, near Honolulu Harbor. Used to be real beautiful ogo from Sand Island before they neutralized the ground out there. I don't know what they did, but the ground changed and there's no more ogo. But there's still some good farm-raised ogo on the Big Island, thank goodness. The best thing about it is its high-iron content. It will supply you more than enough of that vital mineral. Ogo fixes up really nicely for pickling, like in kim chee,

and there's ogo in poke. But I'm sure there are more creative ways in which we'll be able to use it.

I'd also like to see more of our tropical fruits get the attention they deserve. There used to be a lot of soursop grown in the Islands, but you hardly see it anymore. Soursop grows on trees; the fruit has a thin, spiny shell outside and tart, edible pulp inside. A very unique taste. The fruits we do have a lot of, though — like star fruit, lychee, mango, pomelo, pineapple, orange (especially Kona oranges, which must be the sweetest in the world), lemon, lime, strawberry and yellow guava, poha, date, the big Hawaiian avocado (which local folks call "pears," used to be "alligator pears"), mountain apple, and pomegranate, and more yet — you can still use all these varieties in salads and garnishes for great colors and wild tastes.

"THE OLD SAND ISLAND DAYS" OGO PICKLE—"NOT"

48

MAKES 2 ⅓ GALLONS

When I was 15 years old, I picked ogo at Sand Island. The ogo was long and healthy. The building of the sewer ended that. People can remember that ogo, but then they still say, not!

6 pounds fresh ogo
   (edible seaweed), chopped
2 Maui onions, julienned
1 small radish, sliced (optional)
1 ½ cups sugar
1 cup soy sauce

1 cup rice vinegar, available in Asian
   section of markets
½ cup sesame seeds toasted in a dry skillet
1 tablespoon grated fresh ginger
Red chile pepper flakes to taste

IN A LARGE (3-GALLON) CONTAINER, combine all ingredients and mix well. Put mixture into large glass jars and refrigerate 4 to 5 days, turning jars upside down several times. Chill until served.

Approximate nutrient content per ½ cup serving:
35 Calories, 0.5 gram total fat, no saturated fat,
no cholesterol, 230 milligrams sodium, 5 grams
carbohydrate, and 3 grams protein.

A bowl of fresh ogo, or seaweed, captures the essences of both sun and sea.

Nineties Style Potato Salad

50

Makes 18 (½-Cup) Servings

We've got all different things in this salad — crab, uncooked corn kernels that add a little crunchiness. Whew, ono. You never had it like that before? It's the nineties!

2 pounds new Red B (round red boiling)
   potatoes
2 cups shredded crabmeat
½ cup bay shrimps
4 hard-boiled eggs, chopped
1 cup fresh corn kernels
½ cup pitted medium black olives

¼ cup sliced water chestnuts
1 ½ cups chopped fresh spinach
½ cup minced Maui onion
½ cup minced celery
½ cup grated carrots
2 ½ cups mayonnaise
Salt and pepper to taste

Cook potatoes in lightly salted boiling water until fork-tender. Cool, then cut into eighths.

In a large mixing bowl, toss all ingredients lightly to combine. Adjust seasoning with salt and pepper, if necessary.

Approximate nutrient content per serving, based on 1 teaspoon total added salt: 330 Calories, 26 grams total fat, 4 grams saturated fat, 80 milligrams cholesterol, 400 milligrams sodium, 18 grams carbohydrate, and 7 grams protein.

Low-fat tip: Substitute nonfat mayonnaise plus 1 or 2 teaspoons prepared horseradish to achieve 2 grams total fat and 130 Calories per serving.

Bella Mushroom Salad 🍄

Makes 8 (1-Cup) Servings.

l large red bell pepper
4 large portobello mushrooms (6 inches
    in diameter each), stems discarded
2 teaspoons olive oil
Salt and freshly ground black pepper
    to taste
1 bunch arugula, torn in bite-size pieces
    (about 2 cups)
¼ head lollo rosa (red curly) or
    other preferred lettuce, torn in
    bite-size pieces
Grated cheese of choice

Tomato dressing:
    ½ pound plum tomatoes,
        blanched, peeled and seeded
    1 garlic clove
    1 ½ tablespoons fresh orange juice
    1 ½ teaspoons rice vinegar,
        available in Asian section of markets
    1 teaspoon soy sauce
    1 tablespoon chopped fresh mint

Toss together Italian lettuces, beefy portobellos and colorful "bells" with a fat-free plum-tomato dressing — bella!

To prepare bell-pepper strips: Roast pepper directly over a gas flame or as close under a broiler as possible, turning frequently, until charred all over. Put immediately into plastic bag to steam 5 minutes. Use a small sharp knife to peel pepper, and remove stem, seeds and ribs. If desired, rinse and pat dry. Slice in thin strips.

To prepare tomato dressing: Machine process tomatoes and garlic; pour purée into a small bowl. Stir in remaining dressing ingredients.

To prepare portobellos: Arrange mushrooms on a baking sheet; brush completely with oil, and season with salt and pepper. Broil, gill sides down, 2 minutes or until tender and toasty brown on top. Cut in large chunks; keep warm.

To serve: In a large bowl, toss arugula and lollo rosa lettuce with tomato dressing. Mound salad on 4 large plates. Scatter pepper strips and mushroom chunks over top. Sprinkle with cheese.

Curly red lollo rosa lettuce is originally from Italy.

Approximate nutrient content per serving, based on part-skim mozzarella cheese and ¼ teaspoon total added salt: 60 Calories, 2.5 grams total fat, 1 gram saturated fat, 5 milligrams cholesterol, 150 milligrams sodium, 6 grams carbohydrate, and 4 grams protein.

LOMILOMI SALMON WITH A TWIST

MAKES 12 (1/2-CUP) SERVINGS

1 pound salted salmon (brine salmon)

1 cup dried shrimp

Vegetable oil for deep-frying, such as
safflower, cottonseed or corn oil

2 onions, diced

3 ripe medium-size tomatoes, diced

1/2 cup diced green onions

2 cups chopped fresh ogo (edible seaweed)

When you bite into the fried 'opae (shrimp), it's really good, sweet — plus the ogo. This is lomilomi salmon with something to chew on.

SOAK SALMON in fresh water overnight in refrigerator. Just before assembling salad, deep-fry dried shrimp. Heat oil to 350 to 365 degrees. Use a deep-frying basket, if available. Fry shrimp just a few moments or until crunchy; drain on paper towel to remove extra oil.

RINSE OFF EXCESS SALT from soaked salmon, discard skin and bones, and dice into small chunks. In a mixing bowl, combine all ingredients and don't forget "Sam Choy's twist" — the crunchy 'opae shrimp and the ogo. Chill until served.

Approximate nutrient content per serving:
110 Calories, 5 grams total fat, 1 gram saturated fat,
25 milligrams cholesterol, 60 milligrams sodium,
4 grams carbohydrate, and 12 grams protein.

Lower-fat tip: Add 1 tomato and 1 onion, and use only 1/2 pound salmon to achieve 3.5 grams total fat and 80 Calories per serving.

An updated version of lomilomi salmon is served in a traditional-style chief's food bowl.

TURNING LEAF
NORTH COAST
Zinfandel
1992

PUNA PAPAYA AND MAUI ONION DRESSING

54

MAKES ABOUT 3 CUPS

Take overripe Puna papaya and blend it with the sweetness of Maui onions. This simple recipe utilizes the best of two worlds — Puna on the Big Island and Upcountry Maui.

1 ½ small papayas, seeded and peeled
½ small Maui onion
¼ cup rice vinegar, available
    in Asian section of supermarkets
    and in Asian markets

1 tablespoon sugar
1 cup canola oil
Salt and pepper to taste

MACHINE PROCESS PAPAYA, Maui onion, rice vinegar and sugar. With food processor or blender running, add oil in a slow, steady stream. Season with salt and pepper to taste.

Approximate nutrient content per 2-tablespoon serving: 80 Calories, 7 grams total fat, 0.5 gram saturated fat, no cholesterol, 3 milligrams sodium, 3 grams carbohydrate, and no protein.

Low-fat tip: Use 2 medium papaya and only ¼ cup canola oil to achieve 2 grams total fat and 30 Calories per serving.

DILL VINAIGRETTE

MAKES 1 ¼ CUPS

¼ cup rice vinegar, available in Asian
    section of markets
¼ cup fresh dill
2 tablespoons sugar

1 ½ tablespoons Maui onion
2 garlic cloves
Salt and white pepper to taste
¾ cup olive oil

MACHINE PROCESS all ingredients except oil. With food processor or blender running, add oil in a slow steady stream.

Approximate nutrient content per 2-tablespoon serving based on no added salt: 155 Calories, 16 grams total fat, 2 grams saturated fat, no cholesterol, 55 milligrams sodium, 3 grams carbohydrate, and no protein.

Lower-fat tip: Omit olive oil (which reduces quantity to ½ cup dressing) to achieve 30 Calories and no fat per serving.

LIMU LOMILOMI RELISH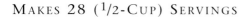

MAKES 28 (1/2-CUP) SERVINGS

2 pounds fresh ogo (edible seaweed),
    chopped in 2- to 4-inch lengths
1 Maui onion, diced
1/2 cup diced green onion
3/4 cup diced fresh tomatoes

3/4 cup sugar
1/2 cup rice vinegar, available in Asian
    section of markets
1 teaspoon minced fresh ginger
1/2 teaspoon salt

Rice vinegar is one of my secret ingredients. The clear Japanese fermented-rice vinegar gives salads, dressings and relishes a mild piquancy.

IN A MIXING BOWL, combine all ingredients and "lomilomi," or mix well. Chill until served.

Approximate nutrient content per serving: 30 Calories, no fat, no cholesterol, 70 milligrams sodium, 7 grams carbohydrate, and 2 grams protein.

KEAHOLE OGO SALAD WITH MISO DRESSING

MAKES 10 (1/2-CUP) SERVINGS

3 cups fresh ogo (edible seaweed)
2 tablespoons diced fresh tomato
2 tablespoons diced onion
2 tablespoons diced green onion
3 tablespoons miso (fermented
    soybean paste), available in Asian
    section of markets

3 tablespoons soy sauce
3 tablespoons sugar
1 tablespoon black sesame seeds (goma),
    toasted in a dry skillet
1 teaspoon sesame oil

Steve Katase of Royal Hawaiian Sea Farms at Keahole on the Big Island raises ogo — a uniquely crunchy, sun-drenched product of Hawai'i.

RINSE OGO and chop in 2-inch lengths. In a medium bowl, combine all ingredients and mix well.

COOKING TIP:

    To toast sesame seeds, stir seeds occasionally in a hot, dry skillet for 3 to 5 miniutes or until lightly browned. Or, roast sesame seeds on a dry baking sheet at 325 degrees until a light, toasty brown, about 10 to 15 minutes. Cool and store in a glass jar.

Approximate nutrient content per serving: 45 Calories, 1.5 grams total fat, no saturated fat, no cholesterol, 490 milligrams sodium, 6 grams carbohydrate, and 3 grams protein.

Ke ʻAwapuhi ʻAi

(Ginger)

58

Previous pages: This Hilo ginger farm raises some of the rhizomes that give the crop a farm value of $5 million per year.

Workers process ginger in Hilo.

Ginger is that smell that makes your mouth water. You know, that sweet, warm "I'm so hungry" smell of teriyaki chicken on the hibachi.

I got hooked on cooking with this spicy herb root while helping my dad in the kitchen. When he cooked with fresh ginger, it was either Bang! with the big cleaver, smashing the root into flat splinters, or chop, chop, chop, mince, mince, mince into diced little pieces. Either way, the oils that were locked in its fibers were released, and you could taste the peppery scent in the air even before Dad added it to the dish. He could do magic. He added his special touch to just about everything—shoyu chicken, chicken long rice, all the stir-fry dishes. It wasn't any fun to peel, but it was worth it.

To me, the perfect flavor marriage is ginger pesto. It's the "best" for chicken. The blend of fresh ginger, cilantro, and scallions really brings out the flavor of the meat. It's really good!

I like the savory-hot taste of ginger so much that I have included this whole chapter of gingered recipes like Ginger Clams with Black Bean Sauce, Spicy Braised Chicken with Ginger, Ginger Steamed Mussels, and Gingered Scallops with Colorful Soba Noodles. These pungent, hearty dishes are so popular that I get requests for the recipes all the time. So here they are. Bang 'em, chop 'em, mince 'em, and enjoy.

GINGER, GINGER STEAMED MUSSELS

MAKES 6 SERVINGS

6 pounds fresh green mussels
2 cups light clam stock
1 cup Sonoma Gallo Chardonnay
2 tablespoons minced fresh ginger
2 tablespoons minced shallots
2 tablespoons chopped fresh parsley
2 tablespoons butter

1 tablespoon chopped fresh garlic
Salt and pepper to taste
1 cup diced and seeded fresh tomatoes
   (about 2 medium)
1/4 cup combination minced green onion
   and minced cilantro

Here's a clear, light broth with a heavy ginger flavor. There's never enough ginger. Try adding just one chile pepper to the broth. Whew, I like this one.

UNDER RUNNING WATER, scrub mussel shells and pull off "beards," or filaments. In a large pot, combine clam stock, wine, ginger, shallots, parsley, butter, garlic, salt and pepper. Bring to a boil, add mussels and adjust seasoning with salt and pepper. Cover and return to a boil until mussel shells open. Transfer mussels with shells to a serving platter.

BOIL LIQUID to reduce to half. Stir in tomato, green onion and cilantro. Pour over mussels and serve. Great with garlic bread.

Approximate nutrient content per serving, based on
1/4 teaspoon total added salt: 180 Calories, 7 grams total
fat, 3 grams saturated fat, 45 milligrams cholesterol,
630 milligrams sodium, 8 grams carbohydrate, and
15 grams protein.

*Lower-fat tip: Omit butter to achieve 3 grams total fat and
140 Calories per serving.*

GINGER CLAMS WITH BLACK BEAN SAUCE

60

MAKES 4 SERVINGS

Just try this simple dish once and you're hooked. Use any kind of clams — cherrystones from the Pacific Northwest, Manila clams or New Zealand clams.

½ tablespoon salted fermented black beans (dau see)
2 tablespoons peanut oil
½ cup ground pork
36 fresh clams in shells, scrubbed and rinsed
½ cup julienned fresh ginger
2 cloves garlic, minced
½ teaspoon minced Hawaiian red chile pepper (or red chile pepper flakes)

1 ½ cups chicken stock
4 tablespoons sherry
¼ cup chopped green onion
2 tablespoons soy sauce
1 tablespoon oyster sauce
1 teaspoon sugar
1 ½ tablespoons cornstarch
3 tablespoons water
½ cup chopped cilantro

SOAK BLACK BEANS in water; then rinse, drain and mash into a paste.

IN A WOK, heat oil on medium-high heat and add pork, clams, ginger, garlic and chile; stir-fry 3 to 4 minutes. Add chicken stock, dau-see paste, sherry, green onion, soy sauce, oyster sauce and sugar. Bring to a boil, reduce heat, then simmer until clams open.

MIX CORNSTARCH and cold water to make a paste; add to clam mixture and stir 1 minute to thicken.

SERVE IN A LARGE BOWL and garnish with cilantro. Goes great with hot steamed rice.

Approximate nutrient content per serving: 310 Calories, 18 grams total fat, 4 grams saturated fat, 50 milligrams cholesterol, at least 1,500 milligrams sodium, 13 grams carbohydrate, and 20 grams protein.

Lower-fat tip: Use lean ground pork and only 1 teaspoon peanut oil to achieve 9 grams total fat and 240 Calories per serving.

LOCAL-STYLE GINGER BRAISED CHICKEN

MAKES 6 SERVINGS

Braise a whole chicken with a little shoyu, ginger, sherry and sugar. The sauce comes out with lots of ginger flavor running through. There's not enough rice in the world to go with it.

3 tablespoons canola oil
1 whole fryer chicken
2 stalks green onion
2 or 3 slices (1/4 inch each) fresh ginger, bruised
3 tablespoons sherry

1/2 cup soy sauce
2 cups fat-free chicken stock
1/2 teaspoon salt
1 tablespoon sugar
Cilantro sprigs

IN A LARGE heavy pan, heat oil on medium-high heat and brown whole chicken quickly on all sides. Add remaining ingredients except cilantro. Bring to a boil, reduce heat, then simmer covered for 20 to 30 minutes. Add sugar and simmer covered for 10 to 15 minutes more.

CUT CHICKEN in serving-size pieces and arrange in a serving bowl. Strain sauce and pour over chicken. Garnish with cilantro.

VARIATION: In place of green onion, substitute 2 crushed garlic cloves and a pinch red chile pepper flakes. Also, for richer ginger flavor, add up to 10 slices bruised ginger.

Approximate nutrient content per serving: 470 Calories, 33 grams total fat, 8 grams saturated fat, 155 milligrams cholesterol, at least 1,700 milligrams sodium, 4 grams carbohydrate, and 36 grams protein.

🌶 Low-fat tip: Substitute 6 skinless chicken-breast halves and use only 2 teaspoons canola oil to achieve 3 grams total fat and 180 Calories per serving.

GINGER SHOYU PORK

MAKES 8 SERVINGS

1 tablespoon canola oil
2 cloves garlic, crushed
4 pounds lean boneless pork butt
   (all visible fat trimmed),
   cut in 3-inch cubes

1 cup soy sauce
1 cup fat-free chicken stock
1 cup packed brown sugar
4 slices (1/2 inch each)
   fresh ginger, bruised

This is like shoyu chicken — real simple, real easy. You have to pay attention, though, to stir it now and then — it's that easy.

IN A 5-QUART POT, heat oil on medium-high heat, add garlic and brown pork 3 to 5 minutes. Add remaining ingredients. Bring to a boil, reduce heat, then simmer uncovered for 1 hour or until tender, turning pork occasionally.

SERVE WITH HOT RICE and steamed vegetables, Chinese cabbage or mustard cabbage.

Approximate nutrient content per serving: 410 Calories, 12 grams total fat, 4 grams saturated fat, 125 milligrams cholesterol, at least 2,000 milligrams sodium, 27 grams carbohydrate, and 45 grams protein.

Lower-fat tip: Use only 3 pounds lean pork butt and 1 teaspoon canola oil to achieve 9 grams total fat and 340 calories per serving.

SPICY BRAISED CHICKEN WITH GINGER

MAKES 6 SERVINGS

2 tablespoons olive oil

2 tablespoons sesame oil

1 whole fryer chicken

1/4 cup soy sauce

1/4 cup sherry

6 slices (1/4 inch each) fresh ginger, bruised

2 stalks green onions, cut in 2-inch pieces

3 whole star anise

1 tablespoon Sichuan peppercorns

1 1/2 tablespoons sugar

6 sprigs cilantro

This dish not only has a clean taste, but also spices your mouth up. It takes you away from basic, round flavors; instead, you get a sharp (flavor) point.

IN A LARGE heavy pan, heat olive oil and sesame oil. Brown whole chicken on all sides. Add soy sauce, sherry, ginger, green onions, star anise and peppercorns. Bring to a boil, reduce heat, then simmer on very low heat 40 minutes or until almost done, turning once or twice for even coloring.

ADD SUGAR and simmer covered for 5 minutes more. Cool slightly, then cut chicken in serving-size pieces. Garnish with cilantro.

Approximate nutrient content per serving: 490 Calories, 35 grams total fat, 9 grams saturated fat, 155 milligrams cholesterol, 740 milligrams sodium, 5 grams carbohydrate, and 33 grams protein.

Lower-fat tip: Substitute skinless chicken breasts and use only 1 tablespoon each olive oil and sesame oil to achieve 6 grams total fat and 210 Calories per serving.

MISO MISO BONELESS CHICKEN THIGHS WITH GINGER

66

MAKES 4 SERVINGS

Boneless chicken thighs are always tasty and moist. And, what a flavor blend — almost like teriyaki, but with miso and ginger. I call it comfort food.

8 deboned chicken thighs

3 tablespoons canola oil

4 tablespoons red miso (fermented soybean paste), available in Asian section of markets

6 tablespoons sake (Japanese rice wine)

6 tablespoons sugar

4 tablespoons fat-free chicken stock

3 tablespoons minced fresh ginger

3 tablespoons chopped green onions

2 tablespoons mirin (glutinous-rice wine)

2 garlic cloves, minced

IN A WOK, heat oil on medium-high heat and brown chicken fillets. Combine remaining ingredients and pour over chicken. Cover pan and simmer 6 minutes or until done.

P.S. WATCH OUT, RICE!

Approximate nutrient content per serving: 650 Calories, 40 grams total fat, 9 grams saturated fat, 160 milligrams cholesterol, 800 milligrams sodium, 27 grams carbohydrate, and 36 grams protein.

Lower-fat tip: Remove chicken skin and use only 1 tablespoon canola oil to achieve 10 grams total fat and 350 Calories per serving.

DEGLAZING GRACE

My favorite recipe would have to be beef stew. I like beef stew — it's easy and it's all in one pot. There's just something homey and basic about it, something simple, and reliable, and wholesome, and true.

In Hawai'i, folks have different styles of cooking beef stew. My secret comes from my dad. I start out by browning the meat really well with garlic, onions, and celery until everything's dark brown. Then I add the stock and let the mixture simmer. All you're doing at this point is deglazing — heating stock in the pan and stirring to loosen the browned morsels of food on the bottom. This process sets the tone for what I do throughout all of my cooking.

For example, after you roast chicken or beef, you pull it out of the oven with all those dark pan drippings encrusted around the pan. Then, you add the stock or water or wine and bring it to a boil to deglaze the pan of those deep, rich flavors.

By browning I don't mean burning. I keep browning the stew meat, garlic, onions, and celery until the beef and vegetable essences are all blended into one. Then I add the stock and it releases that essence

A lot of people boil the stew meat first. They don't pay attention to that

good beginning. And that's why I think beef stew offers that "Cooking 101" lesson for good flavor and good taste. In all the braised dishes, you want to do the same thing. It's really critical if you want to get all those flavors out.

My dad taught me to feel free to cook with no restrictions. Go for it and add whatever you think might work, and that's good advice for beef stew.

The first time I applied that notion outside of home was as a freshman in culinary arts classes at Kapi'olani Community College (KCC). Our instructor, who remains one of my idols in the cooking world, was George Ah Hoy. On our first day of cooking we students were to make lunch for the school kids. We had all the stuff planned that morning for the short-order menu — stir-fry, rice, fried rice, soup, dessert. The student chefs stood around bright-eyed, holding napkins, wearing clean aprons with towels

on the side. Everyone looked back and forth saying, "What's next? What's next?"

I just went in, threw oil in the wok, threw in the Hawaiian salt (crackle!), threw in ginger and garlic, the won bok cabbage, stir-fried a bit of soy sauce and a little oyster sauce. The other students got concerned, saying, "Oh, maybe too much of that."

I said, "Nah, that's how my dad cooks. No worry. No worry."

Then George Ah Hoy walked in. "This guy's cooked before," he said.

Two other instructors at KCC became my idols — Mrs. Arline Hoe, the legend of the school; and Walter Schiess, former pastry chef at the Royal Hawaiian Hotel.

All these good folks, like my dad, taught and retaught the beef stew rule to get in there and cook, no stand around, no overprepare, just start throwing things into the pan!

GINGERED SCALLOPS WITH COLORFUL SOBA NOODLES

MAKES 6 SERVINGS

1 ¹/2 pounds scallops
2 teaspoons canola oil

Marinade:
   1 ¹/2 tablespoons dry white wine
   1 ¹/2 tablespoons orange juice
   1 tablespoon minced ginger
   1 tablespoon minced red bell pepper
   (or 1 Hawaiian red chile pepper, seeded
   and minced)
   1 tablespoon minced yellow bell pepper
   1 tablespoon chopped fresh basil
   1 tablespoon minced cilantro
   ¹/2 teaspoon sugar
   Salt and white pepper to taste

Pasta Mixture:
   ¹/2 pound soba (Japanese thin brown
        wheat noodles)
   12 fresh spinach leaves
   ¹/2 cup julienned carrots
   ¹/2 cup julienned red bell pepper
   ¹/2 cup julienned zucchini
   12 fresh basil leaves
   1 tablespoon minced cilantro
   1 tablespoon soy sauce
   1 tablespoon olive oil
   1 teaspoon sesame seed oil
   1 teaspoon minced garlic

This soba salad has beautiful vegetable colors — carrot curls, zucchini curls, red bell pepper strips, plus scallops poached in ginger stock.

IN A BOWL, combine marinade ingredients and marinate scallops.

COOK SOBA according to package directions; drain. In a large mixing bowl, combine soba with remaining pasta-mixture ingredients. Toss like a Caesar salad.

IN A SKILLET, heat oil over medium heat and sauté scallops 1 ¹/2 minutes on each side; do not overcook. Pour scallops and juices right over soba.

Approximate nutrient content per serving, based on ¹/4 teaspoon total added salt: 300 Calories, 6 grams total fat, 0.5 gram saturated fat, 35 milligrams cholesterol, 520 milligrams sodium, 36 grams carbohydrate, and 27 grams protein.

70

BRAISED GINGER HONEY CHICKEN

MAKES 6 SERVINGS

A lot of people cook Chinese dishes and add molasses or caramelize with brown sugar, then add stock. Here, I try one with honey…

1 whole fryer chicken (3 pounds)
1 stalk green onion, cut in 1/2-inch pieces
3-inch piece fresh ginger, minced
4 tablespoons canola oil
1/2 cup sherry

2 tablespoons honey
1/2 cup fat-free chicken stock
2 tablespoons soy sauce
1 teaspoon salt
8 sprigs cilantro

IN A HEAVY WOK or pan, heat oil on medium-high heat and stir-fry ginger and green onion a few times. Brown chicken on all sides 6 to 8 minutes; drain off excess oil.

COMBINE REMAINING ingredients except cilantro and pour slowly over chicken. Bring to a boil, reduce heat, then simmer covered for 40 minutes or until done, basting frequently.

USE A CLEAVER to chop chicken, bones and all, in 2-inch pieces. Serve with steamed rice.

Approximate nutrient content per serving: 440 Calories, 28 grams total fat, 6 grams saturated fat, 125 milligrams cholesterol, 830 milligrams sodium, 8 grams carbohydrate, and 33 grams protein.

Low-fat tip: Use skinless chicken-breast halves and only 2 teaspoons canola oil to achieve 3 grams total fat and 200 Calories per serving.

COLD CHICKEN TOSSED WITH FRESH GINGER PESTO

MAKES 6 SERVINGS

2 cups water
1/2 cup chopped cilantro
1-inch piece ginger, crushed
2 cloves garlic, minced
1/2 teaspoon salt
6 skinless boneless chicken-breast halves

Fresh Ginger Pesto:
   1/2 cup canola oil
   1/2 teaspoon salt
   1/4 cup minced fresh ginger
   1/4 cup minced green onion
   1/4 cup lightly packed cilantro, minced
   1/2 cup finely chopped
       macadamia nuts
   2 tablespoons minced shallots
   1/8 teaspoon white pepper

Ginger pesto and chicken make a perfect marriage of flavors. How can you beat that? It's fresh-tasting. Every bite just explodes with flavors.

TO POACH CHICKEN: In a medium pot, bring to a boil the water, cilantro, ginger, garlic and salt. Add chicken, reduce heat, then simmer 6 minutes or until tender. Remove chicken from water and chill.

TO PREPARE PESTO: In a small saucepan, heat oil and salt 2 or 3 minutes; cool. Stir in remaining pesto ingredients. Makes 1 cup.

CUT CHICKEN in 1-inch-wide strips and toss with Fresh Ginger Pesto. Great with crisp assorted greens in a salad or with hot steamed rice.

Approximate nutrient content per serving: 370 Calories, 27 grams total fat, 2.5 grams saturated fat, 70 milligrams cholesterol, 440 milligrams sodium, 3 grams carbohydrate, and 28 grams protein.

Lower-fat tip: Use only 1/4 cup canola oil and 1/4 cup macadamia nuts to achieve 14 grams total fat and 250 Calories per serving.

GINGERED LOBSTER

72

MAKES 2 SERVINGS

Enhance Hawaiian spiny lobster caught off Waimea, O'ahu, or Maine lobster raised at Keahole point, Big Island, with the classic trio of ginger, garlic and soy sauce.

2 tablespoons canola oil
2 tablespoons sliced fresh ginger
2 tablespoons minced garlic
1 whole lobster, cut in 6 pieces
2 tablespoons soy sauce

1 cup chicken stock
1 tablespoon cornstarch
2 tablespoons cold water
2 tablespoons chopped green onion tops

IN A HEAVY SKILLET, heat oil over medium heat and cook lobster, ginger and garlic 2 minutes. Add soy sauce and stock, cover and cook 8 to 10 minutes. Mix cornstarch and cold water to make a paste; stir in to thicken. Toss in green onions.

SERVE IMMEDIATELY over rice or noodles.

Approximate nutrient content per serving: 340 Calories, 17 grams total fat, 1.5 grams saturated fat, 105 milligrams cholesterol, at least 1,600 milligrams sodium, 12 grams carbohydrate, and 34 grams protein.

🌿 *Low-fat tip: Use only 1 teaspoon canola oil in a nonstick skillet when cooking lobster (add water, if necessary, to prevent burning) to achieve 6 grams total fat and 240 Calories per serving.*

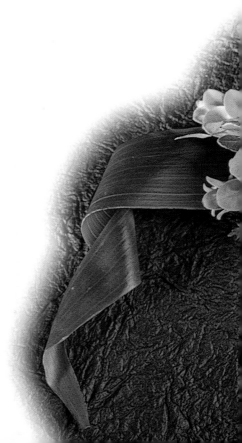

KA IPUHAO PĀKE

(WOK)

I like using a wok. It's versatile and easy to maneuver. You can use a little oil to sear, hardly any oil to stir-fry. You can steam or braise, or fill it with oil and deep-fry. A wok makes cooking so much fun. You can take it straight from the stove to a hot pad on the table, and serve out of it. It cooks food quickly and cooks it all together. (Less dishes and pans to clean.)

Stainless steel woks are good. A lot of pans are now coated with Teflon, but after a few months of use, you look at it and go, "Where's all the Teflon gone?" My favorite pan is a hand-held wok. They're very easy to care for. After using mine, I like to rub it with a little oil to keep it shined and well seasoned. I am so hooked on woks that I'm thinking of coming out with a signature line of hand-held ones.

Stir-fried Lobster and Tomatoes with Black Beans.

If you don't have a wok already and are thinking of purchasing one, make sure that it's the right size for you. The right weight is important, too. Lift it and pretend you are flipping a flapjack. It should be light enough so you don't feel like you're lifting weights or working out.

It's a lot of fun to experiment. Use the recipes as they are or play around with them. Wok cooking is pretty forgiving. Wat su wok (Lots of Luck)!

WOK-FRIED LOBSTER WITH THICK SOY

MAKES 8 TO 10 SERVINGS

1 stalk green onion, minced
2 or 3 slices (1/16 inch each) fresh ginger, bruised
1 tablespoon cornstarch
2 tablespoons sherry
2 tablespoons chicken stock at room temperature

3 tablespoons canola oil
1 lobster (2 pounds), cut in 8 pieces
2 tablespoons thick soy sauce (like molasses), available in Asian markets
1 teaspoon sugar

Just dip lobster in that thick soy and wok-cook it real quick. The flavor that comes out is amazing. It takes lobster to another level.

COMBINE GREEN ONION, ginger, cornstarch, sherry and chicken stock; mix well. Gently toss lobster in mixture to coat and marinate 15 minutes, turning occasionally.

IN A WOK, heat oil over medium-high heat. Stir-fry lobster 2 minutes or until it starts to brown. Add thickened soy and sugar, and stir-fry 1 minute to blend flavors.

SERVE IMMEDIATELY with hot rice.

Approximate nutrient content per serving, based on 8 servings: 190 Calories, 7 grams total fat, 0.5 gram saturated fat, 80 milligrams cholesterol, at least 850 milligrams sodium, 6 grams carbohydrate, and 24 grams protein.

Lower-fat tip: Use only 1 tablespoon canola oil in a nonstick wok (add water, if necessary, to prevent burning) to achieve 4.5 grams total fat and 170 Calories per serving.

The wok lineup awaits duty in the kitchen at Sam Choy's Diamond Head.

Wok Stir-Fried Chicken with Sweet Peppers and Onions

Makes 4 Servings

Jumping, stirring, mixing, pouring out, adding in — that's what makes wok cooking exciting. If you can't play the game, at least dress the part: A wok makes cooking look good.

2 chicken breasts or 2 whole chicken legs (thighs plus drumsticks)
2 tablespoons canola oil
2 red bell peppers, julienned
1/2 onion, julienned
2 tablespoons oyster sauce
1/2 teaspoon salt
Pinch white pepper
1/4 cup chicken stock
3 sprigs cilantro

Marinade:
1 tablespoon soy sauce
1 teaspoon canola oil
1/2 teaspoon sugar

Remove skin and bone from chicken, and julienne the meat. Combine marinade ingredients and marinate chicken.

In a wok, heat oil and stir-fry chicken 1 minute or until slightly browned; remove from pan. Stir-fry bell peppers and onions 1 minute. Season with oyster sauce, salt and pepper; stir-fry 1 minute more. Return chicken to wok along with stock. Cook covered for 2 or 3 minutes over medium heat.

Garnish with cilantro. Serve immediately. Great over hot steamed rice.

Approximate nutrient content per serving, based on chicken breast: 230 Calories, 10 grams total fat, 1 gram saturated fat, 70 milligrams cholesterol, 970 milligrams sodium, 6 grams carbohydrate, and 29 grams protein.

Low-fat tip: Use only 2 teaspoons canola oil to stir-fry chicken (add water, if necessary, to prevent burning) to achieve 5 grams total fat and 190 Calories per serving.

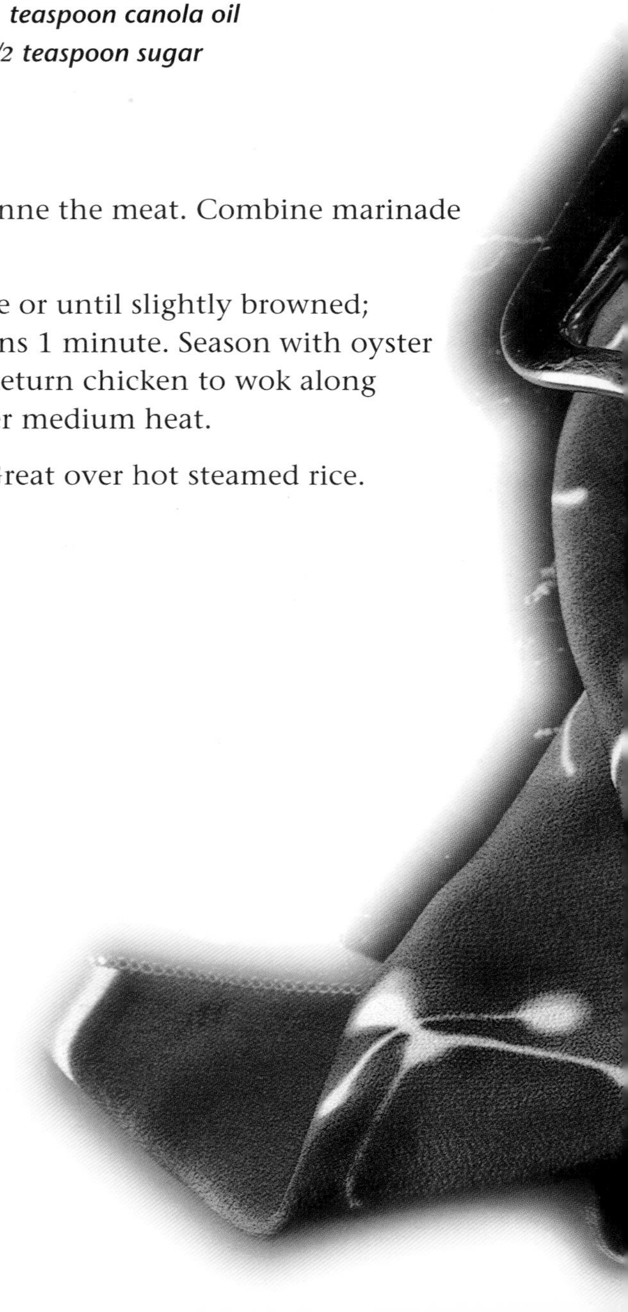

WOK THE CHICKEN WITH EGGPLANT & HOT PEPPERS

80

MAKES 4 SERVINGS

This dish is almost like ma-po tofu, a Chinese favorite recipe where all the ingredients are cooked together like mush. We've got the spicy eggplant with the chicken and hot peppers in there. Real good. I like this one.

2 skinless, boneless whole chicken legs
   (thighs plus drumsticks)
1 tablespoon soy sauce
1 tablespoon sherry
1 tablespoon cornstarch
1 teaspoon sugar
4 tablespoons canola oil

2 fresh chile peppers, seeded and minced
2 or 3 slices ($1/16$ inch each) fresh
   ginger, minced
1 garlic clove, minced
$1/4$ cup chicken stock
1 eggplant, cut in strips

THINLY SLICE CHICKEN, then cut in strips. Combine soy sauce, sherry, cornstarch and sugar; toss chicken in mixture to coat.

IN A WOK, heat 2 tablespoons of the oil and stir-fry chiles until they change color; remove to a plate. Heat remaining 2 tablespoons oil, and stir-fry chicken 1 minute or until it loses pinkness. Stir in ginger and garlic. Add chicken stock and eggplant, and return chiles to wok. Cook, stirring, 2 to 4 minutes to heat through and blend flavors.

SERVE IMMEDIATELY.

Approximate nutrient content per serving: 240 Calories, 16 grams total fat, 1.5 grams saturated fat, 50 milligrams cholesterol, 350 milligrams sodium, 8 grams carbohydrate, and 15 grams protein.

Lower-fat tip: Use only 1 tablespoon canola oil in a nonstick wok to achieve 6 grams total fat and 150 Calories per serving.

WOK SPICY TOFU

MAKES 6 SERVINGS

1 (20-ounce) block firm tofu
3 tablespoons canola oil
4 ounces ground chicken or turkey
2 teaspoons cornstarch
2 teaspoons cold water
1 stalk green onion, chopped
Cilantro
1 teaspoon sesame oil

Sauce:
1 cup chicken stock
2 tablespoons soy sauce
1 tablespoon bottled black-bean sauce
  with chile, available in Asian markets
1 teaspoon chopped garlic
1 teaspoon salt or to taste
1/2 teaspoon chopped fresh ginger

Tofu is really interesting. You can do so many things with it. You could leave the whole tofu in a block and pour the spicy sauce over it and just dig in.

CUT TOFU in 1/2-inch cubes and blanch 30 seconds in boiling water.

IN A WOK, heat oil and stir-fry ground chicken until browned well. Add sauce ingredients and tofu; boil 3 minutes. Mix cornstarch and water to make a paste; add to wok and stir to thicken.

GARNISH with green onion, cilantro and sesame oil drizzled over all.

Approximate nutrient content per serving: 250 Calories, 18 grams total fat, 2.5 grams saturated fat, 15 milligrams cholesterol, at least 1,000 milligrams sodium, 6 grams carbohydrate, and 20 grams protein.

Lower-fat tip: Substitute a lite, or lower-fat, tofu and use only 2 tablespoons canola oil to achieve 10 grams total fat and 150 Calories per serving.

SESAME GINGER SNAP PEAS

MAKES 8 SERVINGS

1 ¹/₂ pounds fresh snap peas
Vegetable oil for deep-frying, such as
　safflower, cottonseed or corn oil
4 tablespoon sesame oil
2 tablespoons minced fresh ginger
2 medium cloves garlic, minced
1 ¹/₂ teaspoons minced green onion

2 tablespoons minced smoked pork
2 tablespoons soy sauce
2 teaspoons rice vinegar, available
　in Asian section of supermarkets
2 teaspoons brown sugar
2 teaspoons cornstarch
¹/₄ cup chicken stock at room temperature
Black sesame seeds (goma)

*When I hear "snap peas"
I think of sweet, crispy,
tender sugar snap peas
speckled with black
goma (sesame) seeds,
with a hint of ginger. . .*

IN A WOK or pan, heat vegetable oil until it is very hot,
　about 365 degrees. Blanch peas in oil 30 seconds. Drain on
paper towels.

IN A SEPARATE WOK, heat sesame oil and sauté ginger, garlic,
　green onion and pork 4 minutes. Add soy sauce, vinegar and brown
　sugar, and bring to a boil. Mix cornstarch and chicken stock to dissolve
cornstarch; stir mixture into wok to thicken. Fold in snap peas.

GARNISH with black sesame seeds that have been toasted in a dry skillet.
Goes great with tofu.

Approximate nutrient content per serving, based on
2 teaspoons black sesame seeds: 140 Calories, 11 grams
total fat, 1.5 grams saturated fat, 5 milligrams cholesterol,
300 milligrams sodium, 8 grams carbohydrate, and
4 grams protein.

*Lower-fat tip: Steam snap peas instead of deep-frying and
use only 2 tablespoons sesame oil to achieve 5 grams total fat
and 90 Calories per serving.*

WOK PORK, PINEAPPLE BARBECUE SAUCE AND LYCHEES

84

MAKES 6 SERVINGS

Why not add lychees to pineapple barbecue sauce — they have the same fruity flavor. That's what makes eating exciting: You educate your tastebuds to go beyond.

³/4 cup bottled Sam Choy's Kona Cuisine Hawaiian Pineapple Barbecue Sauce or ³/4 cup of the recipe below

2 tablespoons sherry

1 tablespoon soy sauce

1 or 2 slices (¹/16 inch each) fresh ginger, minced

1 tablespoon cornstarch

3 tablespoons cold water

2 tablespoons canola oil

12 ounces leanest pork loin, very thinly sliced

1 cup canned lychee fruit plus ¹/2 cup reserved syrup

IN A CUP, combine sherry, soy sauce and ginger. In another cup, mix cornstarch and cold water to form a paste.

IN A WOK, heat oil on medium-high heat and stir-fry pork 1 minute or until it loses pinkness. Add sherry-soy mixture and stir-fry 30 seconds to blend.

ADD SAM CHOY'S Kona Cuisine Hawaiian Pineapple Barbecue Sauce and the lychees. Cover and cook 2 minutes on medium heat. Add lychee juice and stir gently. Stir in cornstarch paste, a little at a time, to thicken. Serve immediately.

Approximate nutrient content per serving: 220 Calories, 8 grams total fat, 1.5 grams saturated fat, 35 milligrams cholesterol, 360 milligrams sodium, 24 grams carbohydrate, and 13 grams protein.

🍴 *Low-fat tip: Use only 2 teaspoons canola oil in a nonstick wok to achieve 5 grams total fat and 190 Calories per serving.*

HAWAIIAN PINEAPPLE BARBECUE SAUCE

MAKES 3 ³/4 CUPS

1 can (4 oz.) crushed pineapple

¹/2 cup pineapple juice

¹/4 cup vinegar

1 cup brown sugar

1 cup ketchup

2 tablespoons soy sauce

2 tablespoons prepared mustard

1 cup onion, minced

IN A MEDIUM SAUCEPAN, bring all ingredients to a boil, reduce heat and simmer 1 hour. Cool and refrigerate until ready to use.

Approximate nutrient analysis per 2 tablespoon serving: 45 Calories, no fat, no cholesterol, 170 milligrams sodium, 11 grams carbohydrate, and 0.5 grams protein.

DECADE OF THE CHEF

My life is like a wok stir-fry with all these ingredients: a healthy business, tasty travel, savory food events, a tantalizing TV cooking show, and piquant promos for my last cookbook — all spiced by the support and stability of my extended family.

Every morning I'm up at 5:00 or 5:30, when I telephone mainland contacts about upcoming food events and projects. By 8:30 a.m. I'm in the Kona headquarters of Sam Choy's Restaurants planning my culinary projects.

I travel to food programs at the invitation of chefs, restaurants, hotels, and business groups around the world — Raffles Hotel in Singapore, Regent Hotel in Hong Kong, and the James Beard House. I was one of six chefs featured at the 1996 Academy Awards party hosted by Whoopi Goldberg at Planet Hollywood. There I met celebrities like Sugar Ray Leonard, Danny Glover, and Charlie Sheen. And everywhere I get to meet a lot of great chefs.

In the nineties the chefs not only make people happy, but generate excitement when they headline fund-raisers. Chefs and their properties donate to every major fund-raiser, benefiting various groups from the ballet to the art guild. In the early sixties through the mid-seventies, musical performers did this. Today chefs lead the way. Celebrity chefs are a drawing card and they generously donate time and food.

I try to appear annually at the gourmet gala for Big Brothers/Big Sisters of Honolulu. This year we invited "new world cuisine" chef Allen Susser of Chef Allen's in South Florida. Last year we had guest chef Kevin Meeker of Philadelphia Fish & Co. The year before that, we featured guest chef Paul Prudhomme.

Food in Hawai'i today is very, very exciting and it has brought prestige and celebrity to Island chefs. When a "celebrity chef" enters a restaurant or a food event, there is immediate recognition.

These chefs, along with talented young newcomers, are introducing the new recipes of Hawai'i, bringing national recognition to these foods. They are creating dishes that use Hawai'i's fresh, exportable produce and seafoods that are distinctive and delicious. The growing interest in Island foods is creating a much-needed boost to our diversified agriculture and fishing industries.

For example, I prepared seared broadbill, or "shutome," for a Washington D.C., program. I also prepared five different poke stylings. For the poke, I brought 200 pounds of fresh Island fish, plus 25 pounds of ogo seaweed. I figured there'd be a little too much poke. However, when I introduced it as "Island fish tartare," the people went nuts. It was unbelievable. We ran out of poke.

Back home my staff and I always challenge ourselves to give everyone not only the true taste of Hawai'i, but the true feeling as well, what we grew up with, that spirit of "Hele mai 'ai, hele mai 'ai" — Come in and eat!

I think that's another thing, besides the range of cultural cuisine we have to choose from, that gives Island chefs an advantage in the world of cooking. Everywhere I go, when people hear I'm from Hawai'i, they literally beam. There's a magic about the place as well as magic in our foods.

And the future looks to be very bright. But let's savor the nineties for a while. After all, it's The Decade of the Chef!

Heating it up in a supermarket for a TV demo.

GARLIC SHRIMP WITH SPINACH, RED PEPPERS & OYSTER MUSHROOMS

MAKES 10 SERVINGS

Definitely the best of the best: Not only is this an elegant dish, but the flavors are great. The juice from the shrimp goes into the oyster mushrooms, along with the garlic from the spinach…

3 large red bell peppers
3 bunches fresh spinach, preferably left whole, rinsed well
8 tablespoons olive oil
12 ounces sliced oyster mushrooms
6 large cloves garlic, minced
1 tablespoon finely chopped Hawaiian red chile pepper or to taste

1 ¼ pounds medium shrimp (31 to 35 pieces per pound), peeled and deveined
2 tablespoons chopped cilantro
Salt and pepper to taste

CHAR THE BELL peppers over a gas flame or under a broiler until skin on all sides is blackened. Place peppers in a plastic bag 10 minutes; then peel, quarter and seed peppers. Arrange peppers on a platter.

IN A LARGE HEAVY SKILLET, heat 4 tablespoons of the oil over medium heat and saute mushrooms and spinach until tender, about 6 to 8 minutes. Season with salt and pepper. Arrange on platter with bell peppers.

IN THE SAME SKILLET, heat remaining 4 tablespoons oil over medium-high heat and saute garlic, chile, shrimp, salt and pepper until the shrimp is done, about 2 to 4 minutes. Fold in cilantro and arrange shrimp over peppers, mushrooms and spinach.

Opposite: Colorful, exotic, island-grown mushrooms are available at firms, such as Kona Mushroom.

Approximate nutrient content per serving, based on 1 teaspoon total added salt: 180 Calories, 12 grams total fat, 1.5 grams saturated fat, 110 milligrams cholesterol, 390 milligrams sodium, 6 grams carbohydrate, and 15 grams protein.

Lower-fat tip: Use a total of only 3 tablespoons olive oil to achieve 5 grams total fat and 125 Calories per serving.

WOK STIR-FRIED ONO AND HAWAIIAN HOT PEPPERS

MAKES 6 SERVINGS

Stir-fry pieces of fresh ono real quick. Add a little stock. Then add hot peppers and zing — you're an instant hero.

1 $^1/_2$ pounds fresh ono (wahoo) or
    other firm fish fillet
1 egg white, lightly beaten
1 tablespoon sherry
1 teaspoon cornstarch
3 tablespoons canola oil
1 garlic clove, minced

$^1/_4$ teaspoon minced ginger
1 green bell pepper, diced
$^1/_2$ cup bean spouts
1 or 2 Hawaiian red chile peppers, minced
1 tablespoon soy sauce
1 teaspoon sugar
$^1/_2$ teaspoon salt

CUT ONO in medium chunks, about 1 by 1 $^1/_2$ inches. Combine egg white, sherry and cornstarch. Add ono and toss to coat.

IN A WOK, heat 1 $^1/_2$ tablespoons of the oil on medium-high heat and lightly brown garlic and ginger. Add ono and stir-fry 2 minutes or until it starts to brown; remove to a plate.

IN THE SAME WOK, heat remaining 1 $^1/_2$ tablespoons oil. Stir-fry bell pepper, bean sprouts and chiles 2 or 3 minutes. Return ono to wok along with soy sauce, sugar and salt. Stir-fry 2 to 4 minutes.

SERVE IMMEDIATELY.

Approximate nutrient content per serving, based on 6 servings: 190 Calories, 10 grams total fat, 1 gram saturated fat, 90 milligrams cholesterol, 420 milligrams sodium, 3 grams carbohydrate, and 21 grams protein.

Lower-fat tip: Use only 1 tablespoon canola oil to achieve 5 grams total fat and 150 Calories per serving.

STIR-FRIED CURRIED SCALLOPS 🦐

MAKES 6 SERVINGS

2 teaspoons cornstarch

1/2 teaspoon sugar

Salt and pepper to taste

2 tablespoons water

2 to 3 tablespoons curry powder

1 medium onion, diced

1 pound fresh scallops

1/2 cup chicken stock

Curry and scallops are like ginger pesto and chicken — another great marriage. Tasting the pureness of the scallop is the important thing.

BLEND CORNSTARCH, sugar, salt, pepper and cold water to form a paste.

IN A DRY WOK over low heat, stir-fry curry powder and onion 2 minutes or until curry odor is pungent. Increase heat to medium and stir-fry scallops briefly to dust with curry. Stir in stock and cook covered for 2 minutes or until done, stirring once or twice. Stir in cornstarch paste to thicken sauce.

SERVE IMMEDIATELY over hot rice.

Approximate nutrient content per serving, based on 1/4 teaspoon total added salt: 90 Calories, 1 gram total fat, no saturated fat, 25 milligrams cholesterol, 300 milligrams sodium, 6 grams carbohydrate, and 13 grams protein.

Lower-fat tip: Eat seconds with a clear conscience.

PAN-FRIED SPICY EGGPLANT

MAKES 4 SERVINGS

3 tablespoons olive oil

2 cloves garlic, minced

2 medium Asian eggplants, peeled and cut
    in 1-inch sections

2 tablespoons soy sauce

1 ½ tablespoons brown sugar

1 tablespoon garlic-chile sauce, available in
    Asian section of markets

1 cup chicken stock

⅛ teaspoon white pepper

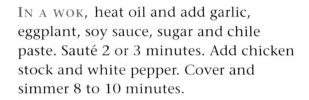

Eggplant and chile paste team up in the wok for an easy, popular favorite that is packed with flavor.

IN A WOK, heat oil and add garlic, eggplant, soy sauce, sugar and chile paste. Sauté 2 or 3 minutes. Add chicken stock and white pepper. Cover and simmer 8 to 10 minutes.

SERVE OVER RICE.

Approximate nutrient content per serving: 150 Calories, 11 grams total fat, 1.5 grams saturated fat, no cholesterol, 940 milligrams sodium, 11 grams carbohydrate, and 3 grams protein.

Low-fat tip: Use only 2 teaspoons olive oil to achieve 3 grams total fat and 80 Calories per serving.

SONOMA RESERVE

TURNING LEAF.
SONOMA COUNTY
Zinfandel
1993

Ke Kapuahi Kōʻala

(Grill)

94

In the summertime everybody grills. The name of the game is usually hibachi…grill…the local g'rilla. Folks dust the cobwebs off the hibachi, set it up on the back porch, and grill three or four times a week. The hibachis stay out all the way through football-tailgating season.

I went to the 1996 Pro Bowl football game and walked through the Aloha Stadium parking lot to check out what people were firing up on their hibachis. There were so many people celebrating over the grill and inviting me to join in that I almost missed the game!

Here's a "dry" marinade that's really great. It's a less-liquid, more potent kind of marinade. Anyway, squirt low-sodium soy sauce into a small bowl. Then add a little sugar, some scallions or green onions. I like fresh cilantro or Chinese parsley, too. Then slice an orange, and squeeze in some of the juice. Do all that, then massage it into the meat and let it sit for about 45 minutes. Throw it in a plastic Ziploc, pack it in ice, and you're ready to go to a tailgate party, the beach, or your friend's backyard.

Nowadays you see more people grilling vegetables. Brush the veggies lightly with olive oil, sprinkle on some garlic salt, then grill and slice. Combine a little soy sauce, sesame oil, and fresh ginger, and pour over the grilled veggies. It's the new wave, gang!

Patti "O" Short Ribs

Makes 4 Servings

2 pounds beef short ribs (1 inch thick each)
Thinly sliced green onions
Sesame seeds toasted in a dry skillet

Marinade:
 1 ½ cups soy sauce
 1 ½ cups brown sugar
 ¼ cup minced ginger

2 tablespoons garlic, minced
2 tablespoons thinly sliced green onions
1 tablespoon sesame oil
1 fresh Hawaiian red chile peppers, seeded
 and minced (¼ teaspoon red chile
 pepper flakes)

When you hear "Patti O," what does it tell you? Patti O … cook the short ribs on the "patio," the lanai. Good, yeah?

COMBINE MARINADE ingredients and marinate ribs 48 hours, turning occasionally. Grill or broil ribs 5 to 10 minutes, turning once. Garnish with green onions and sesame seeds.

Approximate nutrient content per serving, based on
2 teaspoons sesame seeds: 780 Calories, 50 grams total
fat, 20 grams saturated fat, 105 milligrams cholesterol,
540 milligrams sodium, 57 grams carbohydrate, and
25 grams protein.

*Lower-fat tip: Ask the butcher for very lean short ribs to
achieve 15 grams total fat and 440 Calories per serving.*

GOSSAMER BAY
— VINEYARDS —
CALIFORNIA
WHITE ZINFANDEL
1995

YELLOWFIN TUNA WITH LIME-SHOYU MARINADE

MAKES 4 SERVINGS

If you want to send this dish into orbit, start a charcoal grill with kiawe (algaroba) wood. Ono! (delicious)

4 yellowfin tuna ('ahi) fillets (6 ounces each)

Marinade:
  ¼ cup soy sauce
  ¼ cup canola oil
  Juice and grated zest of 1 lime
  2 tablespoons dry sherry

2 tablespoons chopped cilantro
1 tablespoon minced garlic
1 tablespoon brown sugar
2 teaspoons minced fresh ginger
⅛ teaspoon Chinese five-spice powder

COMBINE MARINADE ingredients and marinate fish 1 hour, turning occasionally. Grill or broil fish 10 to 12 minutes, turning once and basting occasionally with marinade.

DO NOT OVERCOOK.

Approximate nutrient content per serving: 340 Calories, 15 grams total fat, 1.5 grams saturated fat, 75 milligrams cholesterol, 990 milligrams sodium, 4 grams carbohydrate, and 42 grams protein.

Lower-fat tip: Use only 1 tablespoon canola oil to achieve 5 grams total fat and 250 Calories per serving.

HOISIN PULEHU PORK CHOPS

MAKES 4 SERVINGS

Hoisin sauce has a tasty ring to it; goes great on pork.

4 lean pork rib chops
  (each 1 ¼ inches thick — 2 pounds total)

Marinade:
  3 tablespoons hoisin sauce
    (Chinese sweet-spicy soybean paste),
    available in supermarkets and
    Asian markets

1 tablespoon soy sauce
2 teaspoons orange juice
1 green onion, sliced
1 teaspoon minced fresh ginger
1 clove garlic, minced
⅛ teaspoon Chinese five-spice powder
Dash ground pepper

COMBINE MARINADE ingredients and marinate pork chops 1 hour. Grill 20 to 30 minutes, basting with marinade to keep meat moist.

DO NOT OVERCOOK.

SERVE WITH ASSORTED grilled vegetables of choice.

COOKING TIP:

Here's a little trick I do: I add citrus — freshly squeezed orange juice or orange concentrate — to my marinades. Slice an orange and squeeze the juice right in, just like for breakfast. I like using citrus because it has a really nice, mellow flavor.

Approximate nutrient content per serving: 310 Calories, 17 grams total fat, 6 grams saturated fat, 80 milligrams cholesterol, 480 milligrams sodium, 6 grams carbohydrate, and 31 grams protein.

Lower-fat tip: Substitute lean center-loin pork chops to achieve 12 grams total fat and 290 Calories per serving.

TAILGATE TERI STEAKS

MAKES 4 SERVINGS

4 lean New York steaks (10 ounces each)
1 tablespoon cornstarch
1 tablespoon cold water
Pineapple wedges
Toasted coconut

Teriyaki sauce:
   2 cups soy sauce
   1 cup mirin
   1 cup water
   1/2 cup brown sugar
   3 teaspoons minced garlic
   3 teaspoons minced ginger
   2 medium oranges, sliced

At one of the University of Hawai'i vs. Brigham Young University-Provo football games, we had live lobsters, steaks and shrimp in the cooler. Pulehu (barbecue) Tailgate Teriyaki on the hibachi; it's always good.

COMBINE TERIYAKI-SAUCE ingredients and reserve 1 cup. In remaining 3 cups sauce, marinate steaks 4 to 6 hours, turning occasionally.

BLEND CORNSTARCH and water to make a paste. Bring reserved marinade to a boil and stir in cornstarch paste to thicken. Grill or broil steaks to desired doneness, basting with thickened sauce.

GRILL OR BROIL pineapple wedges. Garnish each steak with a broiled pineapple wedge and a sprinkling of toasted coconut.

Approximate nutrient content per serving: 640 Calories, 21 grams total fat, 8 grams saturated fat, 160 milligrams cholesterol, at least 3,500 milligrams sodium, 33 grams carbohydrate, and 69 grams protein.

Lower-fat tip: Substitute lean round-tip beef to achieve 13 grams total fat and 580 Calories per serving. Also, consider cutting serving size in half.

HILO MANGO-LILIKO'I-BASIL BARBECUE SHRIMP

101

MAKES 4 SERVINGS

1 pound shrimp (about 16 to 20)
2 large mangoes, each cut
   in 6 large chunks

Marinade:
   ¹/2 cup mango purée
   ¹/2 cup frozen liliko'i concentrate, thawed
   1 tablespoon brown sugar
   1 tablespoon minced fresh basil
   1 tablespoon chopped fresh dill
   1 teaspoon minced fresh ginger
   ¹/2 teaspoon minced garlic

Mango has a flavor of its own. Liliko'i (passion fruit) blends with all that spicy marinated shrimp-on-a-skewer. Sprinkle basil on top...I'm getting hungry already!

PEEL AND DEVEIN SHRIMP, leaving tails on. Combine marinade ingredients and marinate shrimp 1 hour.

ON EACH OF 4 SKEWERS, alternately thread shrimp and mango chunks. Grill or broil kebabs 7 minutes or until shrimp is cooked — turning once and basting occasionally with marinade.

Approximate nutrient content per serving: 220 Calories, 1.5 grams total fat, 0.5 gram saturated fat, 135 milligrams cholesterol, 160 milligrams sodium, 40 grams carbohydrate, and 16 grams protein.

BACKYARD-STYLE BARBECUE RIBS

102

MAKES 4 SERVINGS

I like to marinate ribs, wrap them in foil and throw them in the oven for 45 minutes. Next day throw them on the grill and baste. Watch out, Tony Roma!

2 pounds pork spareribs
  (preferably baby-back ribs)
1/4 cup soy sauce

2 tablespoons minced garlic

2 tablespoons minced fresh ginger

1 tablespoon chili powder

1 tablespoon coarsely ground black pepper

1 teaspoon salt

1/2 cup chopped cilantro

Backyard Barbecue Sauce and Tailgate Teri Sauce, *see page 111*

RUB THE RIBS with soy sauce, garlic, ginger, chili powder, black pepper, salt and cilantro. Wrap ribs in foil and oven bake at 350 degrees 1 hour or until soft and heated through — turning once and basting frequently with barbecue sauce.

TO SERVE, BASTE with a mixture of equal parts Backyard Barbecue Sauce and Tailgate Teri Sauce.

Approximate nutrient content per serving: 520 Calories, 33 grams total fat, 12 grams saturated fat, 130 milligrams cholesterol, at least 1,800 milligrams sodium, 19 grams carbohydrate, and 35 grams protein.

Lower-fat tip: Use leanest pork-loin ribs to achieve 12 grams total fat and 320 Calories per serving.

PHILLY STEAK SAND WITH

When I'm in Philadelphia, usually to visit my friend Chef Kevin Meeker of Philadelphia Fish & Co., we go to places like Tony Luke's. Philly steak sandwiches are famous out there and Tony Luke's sells some of the best. They've also got Jim's, which wins a lot of prizes, and Pat's and Geno's and about four or five other restaurants and delicatessens that are famous for their sandwiches.

But Tony Luke's draws real Italian, mid-America, blue-collar customers. They park anywhere on the four-lane freeway out front, jump off their trucks and order: "Give me the pork steak sand with kohlrabi, provolone cheese, and sweet peppers."

They call them "steak sands," and "with" means "with cheese." "Philly steak sand with" — they say it just like that.

When you go to Pat's, there's a big sign that reads, "If you don't know how to order, practice before you come here." That's because there's a long line of customers and someone who isn't used to it might go, "Uhhh, uhhh." Then the counter person will say, "Honey, the uhhh menu is right there. Practice with that menu and then you come back here." I guess when your sandwiches are so popular you have to do what you can to speed up the ordering process. And people don't seem to mind. It's part of the character of the place, part of its mystique, and maybe the excitement of getting your order right makes the food taste better.

I go to Tony Luke's so often that now, when I arrive there, manager Nick Domenico comes and gets me. "Don't stand in line, Sam," he says. "Come in the back here." They've got my picture right there in the front of their restaurant.

What makes these Philly steak sandwiches so terrific is the way they grill the meats and peppers and onions and how the flavors blend on the bread. It's a tried-and-true recipe. The only thing I can compare it to in the Islands is our trademark plate lunches, which have savory meats blending with rice and macaroni salad, and which our cooks have perfected from generation to generation.

One lesson in this is that delicious doesn't have to be difficult. You can make yourself and your family a great and good-tasting dish without spending a lot of time or energy. So many people have said they liked my cookbooks because the recipes were easy. In this book I've tried to make them even easier. It's getting so people work so much and then they have to come home to cook. We still cook all the time at home. But sometimes after a 12-hour day you find yourself in the kitchen, the kids not listening, the dog biting, your spouse grumbling because you're about to cook the same thing as last time, and that's when you can turn to these recipes. They're not hard. Throw something together. It kind of gives you the feeling like you did something great.

And use the kids to help. This is simple stuff. Let them watch and try. At first they get sticky all over, but be patient. It'll pay off. They learn by doing what you do, they want to be like you, to cook. And they have that enthusiasm, already cooking from the heart. It's amazing. On Fridays at our house my two kids, 10 and 16 years old, they get the cookers and start cooking, and do it in two shakes. Because I never stopped them, you know? I just said, "Well, if you make mess you clean up — just like us."

The three amigos! Here I am with Salevaa Atisanoe and Kevin Meeker at the Tokyo restaurant opening.

Swordfish, Mango and Garlic Bread Kebabs

104

Makes 4 Servings

Swordfish is one of the best fish when it's fresh— very oily and flavorful. Remember not to overcook; grill it just two or three minutes on each side over medium-hot coals.

3 medium mangoes or other fresh fruit
    of choice
1 pound swordfish (shutome) steaks,
    cut in 1 ½ inch cubes
16 cubes (1 ½ inches square) day-old
    Portuguese (or Hawaiian or Easter)
    sweet bread

Basting mixture:
½ cup melted butter
2 tablespoons olive oil
1 tablespoon chopped cilantro
1 teaspoon minced ginger
1 teaspoon minced garlic
Salt and pepper to taste

PEEL AND CUT mangoes into 12 large chunks. On skewers, alternately thread mango, fish and bread, arranging fish between bread and mango chunks.

COMBINE BASTING-MIXTURE ingredients and baste kebabs. Grill kebabs 6 minutes or just long enough to cook fish and to toast — but not burn — the bread. (Or oven bake 15 to 20 minutes at 350 degrees.)

Approximate nutrient content per serving, based on ¼ teaspoon total added salt: 580 Calories, 36 grams total fat, 17 grams saturated fat, 120 milligrams cholesterol, 700 milligrams sodium, 39 grams carbohydrate, and 26 grams protein.

Lower-fat tip: Use only ¼ cup butter and omit olive oil to achieve 18 grams total fat and 410 Calories per serving.

KONA CUISINE SEAFOOD BROCHETTES

MAKES 8 SERVINGS

1 ½ pounds hapu'upu'u
    (grouper or sea bass), see note
¼ of whole fresh pineapple, peeled
1 medium mango, peeled
1 medium bell pepper, seeded
8 slices lean bacon, blanched

8 scallops
6 tablespoons olive oil
6 tablespoons orange juice
1 teaspoon minced fresh basil
Salt and pepper to taste

These elegant, succulent brochettes feature the best elements of Kona — fresh seafood and luscious fruits.

CUT FISH, pineapple, mango and bell pepper into 1-inch cubes. Wrap bacon around scallops like rumaki. On skewers, alternately thread seafood, fresh fruits and bell pepper.

MIX OLIVE OIL and orange juice; marinate brochettes in mixture 30 minutes. Just before grilling, dust brochettes with basil, salt and pepper. Barbecue, basting occasionally with marinade, until cooked.

NOTE: *Can substitute any firm, mild-tasting fish, such as the snappers (onaga, or red snapper; opakapaka, or pink snapper; uku, or gray snapper) or halibut.*

Approximate nutrient content per serving, based on ¼ teaspoon total added salt: 350 Calories, 25 grams total fat, 7 grams saturated fat, 55 milligrams cholesterol, 320 milligrams sodium, 9 grams carbohydrate, and 21 grams protein.

Lower-fat tip: Substitute Canadian bacon and use only 2 teaspoons canola oil to achieve 5 grams total fat and 190 Calories per serving.

Barbecue Beef Short Ribs

MAKES 6 SERVINGS

1 clove garlic, minced
Sea salt and pepper to taste
4 pounds 3-bone beef short ribs

Barbecue sauce:
    2 strips bacon, minced
    1 tablespoon finely chopped onion
    1 can (8 ounces) tomato sauce

$^1/_4$ cup orange juice
2 tablespoons rice vinegar
2 tablespoons brown sugar
1 tablespoon Worcestershire sauce
1 teaspoon red chile pepper flakes

The rub-salt-on-ribs step may be critical. I like to massage spicings into meats and fish, feeling where and how a recipe will take me.

RUB GARLIC, sea salt and pepper on ribs, and let stand while making barbecue sauce.

IN A SAUTÉ PAN, brown bacon and onion. Add remaining barbecue-sauce ingredients. Bring to a boil, reduce heat and simmer, stirring constantly, 10 minutes.

ON AN OPEN GRILL, barbecue ribs while basting frequently with barbecue sauce to keep meat moist. Serve with grilled red potatoes.

Approximate nutrient content per serving, based on $^1/_4$ teaspoon total added salt: 770 Calories, 66 grams total fat, 28 grams saturated fat, 140 milligrams cholesterol, 400 milligrams sodium, 9 grams carbohydrate, and 33 grams protein.

Lower-fat tip: Use very lean beef short ribs to achieve 19 grams total fat and 310 Calories per serving.

TAILGATE ANNIE BARBECUE LEG OF LAMB

MAKES 8 SERVINGS

I remember doing this lamb and people asked, what's that? I said, a little Tailgate Annie. It just had a nice ring to it, so I kept the name. The garlic-shoyu preparation is local-style.

1 boneless leg of lamb (2 1/2 pounds)
3 tablespoons soy sauce

Marinade:
   5 tablespoons soy sauce
   2 tablespoons brown sugar
   2 tablespoons honey

4 cloves garlic, sliced
1 tablespoon cumin
1 teaspoon salt
1/2 teaspoon chili powder

UNROLL LAMB into a flat piece. Use a knife to score any thick sections of meat. Combine marinade ingredients and marinate lamb 4 to 6 hours in refrigerator, turning occasionally. A large resealable plastic bag is good for this step.

TO BARBECUE: Place meat, skin side up, on grill and cook 30 minutes or until browned well, basting with the 3 tablespoons soy sauce. Turn lamb over and cook, skin side down, 20 to 30 minutes more, continuing to baste with soy sauce. Place a loose hood of aluminum foil over meat while the second side cooks.

TO BROIL: Place meat and marinade directly in a shallow roasting pan (without rack), meaty side up. Broil 6 to 8 inches from heat source for 20 to 30 minutes on each side, basting with the 3 tablespoons soy sauce.

SLICE LAMB and arrange on a serving platter. In a saucepan, combine remaining marinade with pan drippings; bring to a boil and pour over sliced lamb.

Approximate nutrient content per serving: 410 Calories, 24 grams total fat, 10 grams saturated fat, 130 milligrams cholesterol, at least 1,200 milligrams sodium, 8 grams carbohydrate, and 39 grams protein.

Lower-fat tip: Use very lean leg of lamb, such as New Zealand lamb, with all visible fat removed, to achieve 9 grams total fat and 260 Calories per serving.

Sweet-Bread Variations for the Grill

Makes Individual Servings

**Sliced Portuguese (or "Hawaiian" or Easter)
    sweet bread**
Aluminum foil

Garlic butter:
    1 stick butter
    2 cloves fresh garlic, diced finely
    Hawaiian (sea) salt

Ginger-cilantro butter:
    1 stick butter
    1 ounce grated fresh ginger

1 ounce chopped fresh cilantro
Hawaiian (sea) salt

Rosemary-garlic olive oil:
    Fresh rosemary
    Finely diced fresh garlic
    Hawaiian (sea) salt
    Olive oil

This is my younger brother Patrick Choy's style of doing French toast. He loves good food, that kid.

Combine ingredients. Spread mixture on bread slices and sprinkle lightly with Hawaiian salt. Wrap in foil and place on hot grill, turning several times until heated well.

Peanut butter-guava:
    Peanut butter
    Guava jam
    Butter

Chocolate chip-banana:
    Chocolate chips
    Banana slices
    Butter

Make a sandwich with each of the ingredients. Butter outside of sweet-bread slices. Wrap in foil, place on hot grill and turn several times.

GRILLED QUESADILLA VARIATIONS

110

MAKES 8 TO 10 SERVINGS

Here are some more specialties from my brother Patrick's "I can grill anything" repertoire.

8- to 10-inch wheat-flour tortillas
Melted butter
Aluminum foil

Grated taco-flavored cheese with
1 preferred combination, as follows:

> *Diced jalapeno peppers and chopped fresh cilantro*

> *Diced tomatoes and chopped fresh cilantro*

> *Diced onions and kalua pig (steamed in an imu, or Hawaiian underground oven)*

> *Chopped green onions and furikake (bottled Japanese seasoned mix of dried seaweed and sesame seeds)*

> *Lomilomi salmon (see recipe on page 53), drained*

> *Chopped green onions and hot chile pepper water (red chiles, water, salt)*

OR 1 sweet grated-cheese combination, as follows:

> *Mild cheddar with cinnamon sugar sprinkled on cheese and on buttered tortilla*

> *Mozzarella and guava jam with sugar sprinkled on cheese and on buttered tortilla*

> *Cheese, diced fresh pineapple and fresh cracked peppercorn with sugar sprinkled on buttered tortilla*

LIGHTLY BRUSH BUTTER on tortilla and place, buttered side down, on 22-inch length of foil. Spread thin, even layer of desired cheese mixture on tortilla. Top with another tortilla buttered on outside; press together slightly. Fold and seal foil. Refrigerate until time to grill.

PLACE WRAPPED quesadilla on hot grill and turn several times to melt cheese and brown tortilla. Remove from grill, open foil and cut in 8 wedges. Serve with favorite salsa.

BACKYARD BARBECUE SAUCE 🍂

MAKES 3 CUPS

1 can (15 ounces) tomato sauce
1 cup brown sugar
1 cup minced onion
¼ cup vinegar
¼ cup honey
1 tablespoon minced garlic
1 tablespoon steak sauce

1 teaspoon liquid smoke
1 teaspoon chili powder
1 teaspoon coarsely cracked black pepper
½ teaspoon cumin
¼ teaspoon dry mustard
1 cinnamon stick

IN A MEDIUM SAUCEPAN, combine all ingredients. Bring to a boil, reduce heat, then simmer 1 hour. Strain and store in refrigerator.

Approximate nutrient content per 2-tablespoon serving:
40 Calories, no fat, no cholesterol, 90 milligrams sodium, 10 grams carbohydrate, and no protein.

TAILGATE TERI SAUCE 🍂

MAKES 2 CUPS

1 cup soy sauce
Juice from 1 medium orange
½ cup mirin
½ cup water

¼ cup brown sugar
1 ½ teaspoons minced garlic
1 ½ teaspoons minced ginger

COMBINE ALL ingredients and blend well.

Approximate nutrient content per 2-tablespoon serving:
30 Calories, no fat, no cholesterol, 660 milligrams sodium, 5 grams carbohydrate, and 2 grams protein.

Na ʻOno ʻOneʻi

(Local Flavors)

Local flavors are the combinations of ethnic ingredients that make me think of home in the Islands. They're the smells and tastes that I remember from small-kid time. They make me want to go back for that second, third, and fourth serving—when I'm down to the last bite and staring into my empty bowl, my stomach saying "full" but I still crave more. Local flavors are locked into ginger and soy sauce, into the crispiness of stir-fry vegetables, into the aroma from herbs like lemon grass.

Some of my favorite local flavors are stew and rice, kalua pork and cabbage, sweet and sour pork, and custard pie. Just the smell of a local-style stew makes me hungry. Local flavors bloom when people take the initiative to make something really 'ono (delicious) and different. I like adding a little citrus to my recipes. Orange concentrate or fresh, it doesn't matter, it adds a real nice, mellow flavor to the dish. Cooking creatively carries on the local tradition of blending and sharing.

I've included in this chapter some of my favorites that define the term "Local Flavor" for me. Remember, it's really important to taste your food while you cook and when you're done cooking, just to make sure it tastes how you like. It's your special touch that will turn these recipes into mouth-watering memories for those you serve.

KAMUELA DRY-RUB TENDERLOIN

MAKES 2 SERVINGS (PICTURED ON PAGES 112/113)

2 beef tenderloin fillets (6 ounces each)
1 teaspoon minced fresh basil
1/4 teaspoon fresh thyme

Dry seasoning salt:
1 teaspoon Hawaiian sea salt
1 teaspoon garlic salt
1 teaspoon paprika
1/2 teaspoon black pepper
1/4 teaspoon onion powder

Tender beef raised in Kamuela, on the slopes of Mauna Kea in the northern part of the Big Island, is enhanced by dry spicings and fast searing. It's a prime-time hit.

IN A SALT SHAKER, combine dry-seasoning-salt ingredients and shake to blend well. Sprinkle seasoning salt over fillets as needed. Reserve remaining seasoning salt for later use, especially on chicken, pork or fish.

SPRINKLE BASIL AND THYME over fillets and massage into meat. In a skillet sprayed with nonstick vegetable-oil cooking spray, pan-fry fillets over medium-high heat 2 1/2 minutes per side (the way I like it) or until done to one's preference.

SERVE WITH PAN-FRIED POTATOES.

Approximate nutrient content per serving: 410 Calories, 30 grams total fat, 12 grams saturated fat, 120 milligrams cholesterol, at least 1,000 milligrams sodium, 1 gram carbohydrate, and 32 grams protein.

Lower-fat tip: Request all lean tenderloin to achieve 15 grams total fat and 290 Calories per serving.

DAD'S FIRST COOKING LESSON—STEAMED MOI WITH LUP CHEONG, GREEN ONION & GINGER

MAKES 4 SERVINGS

1 whole fresh moi (Pacific threadfin —
1 1/2 pounds), scaled and cleaned
(can substitute trout, coho salmon,
halibut fillets)
1/2 teaspoon salt
1 garlic clove, minced

1/2 cup julienned ginger
1 Chinese lup cheong sausage
(1.5 ounces), sliced
2 or 3 tablespoons peanut oil
3 stalks green onions, finely julienned
5 sprigs cilantro
2 tablespoons soy sauce

Bob Kahawai'i told me, ask your dad to teach you how to cook steam' moi — he makes the bes'…. So my dad showed me how.

ON A HEAT-PROOF DISH, place moi and sprinkle with salt, garlic and a little of julienned ginger. Stuff fish with lup cheong and place some lup cheong on top of fish. Steam in a steamer basket 8 to 10 minutes.

IN A SMALL SAUCEPAN, heat peanut oil until it starts to smoke. On top of steamed fish, sprinkle green onions, remaining ginger and cilantro. Pour hot oil over fish and let it sizzle. Top with soy sauce.

Approximate nutrient content per serving, based on 3 tablespoons peanut oil: 350 Calories, 20 grams total fat, 3.5 grams saturated fat, 85 milligrams cholesterol, 940 milligrams sodium, 5 grams carbohydrate, and 37 grams protein.

Lower-fat tip: Use only 1 ounce lup cheong and only 4 teaspoons peanut oil to achieve 13 grams total fat and 290 Calories per serving.

CHICKEN LUʻAU— MY MOTHER'S FAVORITE

118

MAKES 8 (¹/2-CUP) SIDE-DISH SERVINGS

My mom taught me how to do this. Every year we have a big Hawaiian luʻau and the chicken luʻau has to be done the Choy family way.

1 pound luʻau
    (young taro leaves — see note)
3 cups water
1 tablespoon Hawaiian (sea) salt
¹/2 teaspoon baking soda
³/4 pound skinless boneless
    chicken breast, cubed

2 tablespoons butter
¹/2 medium onion, chopped
1 cup chicken stock
1 cup coconut milk
¹/2 teaspoon salt

RINSE LUʻAU and trim off stems and thick veins. In a stockpot, bring water, Hawaiian salt and baking soda to a boil. Add luʻau and cook partially covered for 1 hour. Drain off and squeeze out excess liquid.

IN A LARGE SAUCEPAN, heat butter and sauté onions until translucent. Add chicken and cook 3 minutes, stirring frequently. Add chicken stock, coconut milk, cooked luʻau and salt. Simmer 20 minutes or until chicken is cooked.

NOTE: *Can substitute fresh spinach, which does not need pre-cooking.*

Approximate nutrient content per serving: 160 Calories, 10 grams total fat, 7 grams saturated fat, 35 milligrams cholesterol, at least 400 milligrams sodium, 5 grams carbohydrate, and 14 grams protein.

Lower-fat tip: Use low-fat coconut milk, such as Globe or Trader Joe's (1 gram fat per tablespoon), and only 1 tablepoon butter to achieve 5 grams total fat and 110 Calories per serving.

EASTER ROAST LAMB

MAKES 8 SERVINGS

1 leg (5 pounds, bone in) of lamb roast
Red potatoes, onions, carrots and squash
(optional)

Marinade:
  ½ cup olive oil
  2 tablespoons soy sauce
  1 tablespoon minced onion

1 tablespoon garlic powder
1 tablespoon powdered cumin
1 tablespoon sea salt
1 tablespoon cracked peppercorns
1 teaspoon rosemary
½ teaspoon thyme

An easy, elegant classic — roast leg of lamb arrayed in herbs. You can't go wrong with this.

COMBINE MARINADE and rub into lamb. Marinate several hours in refrigerator, turning lamb frequently.

ON A RACK in a roasting pan, roast the lamb, fat side up, 1 to 1 ½ hours at 350 degrees. Baste with remaining marinade.

GOES GREAT with oven-roasted vegetables, such red potatoes, onions, carrots and squash. Add potatoes and winter squash 50 minutes before end of cooking time; add other vegetables 25 minutes before end of cooking time.

Approximate nutrient content per serving:
540 Calories, 40 grams total fat, 13 grams saturated fat, 150 milligrams cholesterol, at least 1,100 milligrams sodium, 2 grams carbohydrate, and 42 grams protein.

Lower-fat tip: Substitute lean choice or lean New Zealand lamb, and use only 2 tablespoons olive oil to achieve 11 grams total fat and 270 Calories per serving.

EASY LOCAL RIBS

120

MAKES 4 SERVINGS

Oven-braise a local favorite — sweet and sour spareribs packed with pineapple.

3 pounds meaty country-style
    pork spareribs, cut in pieces
3 tablespoons soy sauce
1 teaspoon salt
Dash pepper
Pineapple chunks
Chopped green onion

Sauce:
    1 cup syrup-packed pineapple chunks,
        drained
    1/2 cup packed brown sugar
    1/3 cup ketchup
    1/3 cup vinegar
    2 tablespoons soy sauce
    2 teaspoons grated fresh ginger
    2 cloves garlic, minced

RUB SPARERIBS all over with 3 tablespoons of the soy sauce, salt and pepper. Place ribs, meat side up, in a foil-lined shallow baking or roasting pan, and cover with foil or baking-pan lid. Bake 20 to 25 minutes at 450 degrees. Drain off fat.

COMBINE SAUCE ingredients; pour over ribs. Bake at 350 degrees for 1 hour or until tender, basting occasionally.

GARNISH WITH PINEAPPLE chunks and green onions.

Approximate nutrient content per serving: 570 Calories, 21 grams total fat, 8 grams saturated fat, 130 milligrams cholesterol, at least 2,000 milligrams sodium, 52 grams carbohydrate, and 43 grams protein.

Lower-fat tip: Substitute 1 1/2 pounds boneless lean fresh ham leg, sliced into rib-size strips, to achieve 10 grams total fat and 440 Calories per serving.

CHRISTOPHER'S STIR-FRIED CHICKEN

122

MAKES 4 SERVINGS

*One of my younger son
Christopher's favorites
is stir-fry: stirring the
chicken, adding vegetables,
squirting in cornstarch.
He's got well-formed,
busy hands — hands are
important for a chef.
I like to let my kids cook.
It gets messy if you don't
get after them to clean up.
But how else will they
learn? Too many parents
scare their kids out of
the kitchen.*

2 whole skinless boneless chicken legs
    (thighs plus drumsticks), thinly sliced
2 teaspoons cornstarch
2 tablespoons cold water
3 tablespoons canola oil
8 ounces assorted fresh vegetables of
    choice (carrots, celery, onions, red bell
    pepper, sugar snap peas, Chinese snow
    peas, wing beans, etc.), julienned

1 cup chicken stock
1 tablespoon oyster sauce
Salt and pepper to taste

Marinade:
    2 tablespoons sherry
    1 tablespoon soy sauce
    1/2 teaspoon sugar
    2 slices (1/16 inch each)
        fresh ginger, minced
        1 clove garlic, minced

COMBINE MARINADE ingredients and marinate chicken 1 hour. Combine cornstarch and cold water to form a paste; set aside.

IN A WOK, heat 1 1/2 tablespoons of the oil and stir-fry chicken 2 to 3 minutes; remove to a plate. In same wok, heat remaining 1 1/2 tablespoons oil and stir-fry vegetables. Add chicken stock and oyster sauce, and return chicken to wok. Bring to a boil and adjust seasoning with salt and pepper. Stir in cornstarch paste to thicken. Cook 1 minute more. Pour over hot steamed rice.

Approximate nutrient content per serving, based on no added salt: 220 Calories, 13 grams total fat, 1.5 grams saturated fat, 55 milligrams cholesterol, 720 milligrams sodium, 7 grams carbohydrate, and 16 grams protein.

🍃 *Low-fat tip: Substitute 3 skinless boneless chicken breast halves and use only 1 tablespoon canola oil to achieve 5 grams total fat and 180 Calories per serving.*

BEEF OR PORK LUʻAU STEW

MAKES 12 (9-OUNCE) SERVINGS

2 pounds luʻau (young taro leaves;
   see note)
5 cups water
2 tablespoons Hawaiian (sea) salt
½ teaspoon baking soda

1 tablespoon canola oil
1 cup chopped onions
2 pounds beef brisket or meatiest
   short ribs (see note)
3 cups beef stock

This is always an interesting dish. A lot of the old-timers will automatically have their chile water ready. But you can 'bust' one chile pepper inside (while cooking).

RINSE LUʻAU, and trim off stems and thick veins. In a stockpot, bring to a boil 3 cups of the water, 1 tablespoon of the Hawaiian salt and baking soda. Add luʻau, then cook partially covered for 1 hour. Drain off and squeeze out excess liquid.

IN A POT, heat oil and sauté onions until translucent. Brown beef. Add beef stock and remaining 2 cups water and 1 tablespoon Hawaiian salt. Cook until meat is fork-tender. Add cooked luʻau and simmer 30 minutes more.

NOTE: *Can substitute fresh spinach, which does not need precooking. Also, can substitute meatiest country-style pork spareribs and chicken stock in place of beef and beef stock.*

Approximate nutrient content per serving beef luʻau stew, based on point-cut brisket and 4 teaspoons total added salt: 280 Calories, 22 grams total fat, 8 grams saturated fat, 55 milligrams cholesterol, at least 1,000 milligrams sodium, 6 grams carbohydrate, and 17 grams protein.

Lower-fat tip: Substitute lean flat-cut beef brisket to achieve 7 grams total fat and 170 Calories per serving.

Approximate nutrient content per serving pork luʻau stew, based on 4 teaspoons total added salt: 240 Calories, 16 grams total fat, 5 grams saturated fat, 50 milligrams cholesterol, at least 1,000 milligrams sodium, 6 grams carbohydrate, and 17 grams protein.

Lower-fat tip: Substitute lean country-style pork spareribs and use only 1 teaspoon canola oil to achieve 8 grams total fat and 170 Calories per serving.

Honomalino Lamb with Satay Sauce

Makes 8 Servings

2 to 2 ½ pounds boneless lamb loin

Marinade:
- *2 tablespoons soy sauce*
- *2 tablespoons sugar*
- *2 tablespoons hoisin sauce*
  - *(sweet-spicy soybean-garlic sauce)*
- *2 tablespoons canola oil*
- *1 tablespoon minced garlic*
- *1 tablespoon minced fresh ginger*
- *1 tablespoon cilantro*
- *1 tablespoon minced fresh basil*
- *½ teaspoon red chile pepper flakes*
- *Salt and pepper to taste*

Satay Sauce:

Makes 1½ cups, or 24 (2 tablespoon) servings.
- *2 tablespoons canola oil*
- *½ cup minced onion*
- *1 teaspoon minced ginger*
- *1 teaspoon minced garlic*
- *1 cup minced fresh Thai basil,*
  - *available at Asian groceries*
- *¾ cup peanut butter*
- *2 tablespoons orange juice*
- *2 teaspoons sugar*
- *½ teaspoon chile-garlic sauce (or ¼*
  - *teaspoon red chile pepper flakes),*
  - *available in Asian section of markets*
- *1 ½ cups coconut milk*

This lamb raised on grasses and macadamia leaves in the western part of the Big Island receives Asian embellishments of a spicy marinade and a coconut-laced peanut sauce that give it a special ono taste.

COMBINE MARINADE ingredients and rub mixture into lamb. Marinate 4 to 6 hours in refrigerator, turning lamb occasionally. Broil lamb to desired doneness. Slice and serve with Satay Sauce.

TO PREPARE SATAY SAUCE, heat oil in a saucepan and saute onion, ginger, garlic and basil until onion is translucent. Stir in peanut butter, orange juice, sugar and chile garlic sauce. Cook on low heat 15 minutes, stirring occasionally. Stir in coconut milk and cook until heated through. Cool to room temperature.

Approximate nutrient content per serving lamb only, based on ¼ teaspoon total added salt: 490 Calories, 41 grams total fat, 17 grams saturated fat, 105 milligrams cholesterol, 440 milligrams sodium, 5 grams carbohydrate, and 24 grams protein.

Lower-fat tip: Substitute leanest lamb loin to achieve 12 grams total fat and 260 Calories per serving.

Approximate nutrient content per 2-tablespoon serving of Satay sauce: 90 Calories, 8 grams total fat, 3.5 grams saturated fat, no cholesterol, 40 milligrams sodium, 3 grams carbohydrate, and 2 grams protein.

Lower-fat tip: Use low-fat coconut milk, such as Globe or Trader Joe's (1 tablespoon fat per tablespoon), and only 1 teaspoon canola oil to achieve 5 grams total fat and 60 Calories per serving.

NORTH SHORE HAM HOCKS WITH MONGO BEANS AND EGGPLANT

126

MAKES 12 (9-OUNCE) SERVINGS

Filipinos on the North Shore used to always do pork with mongo beans. It is one of those great dishes where we'd look in the rice pot and ask, "Do we have enough?"

1 cup dried split mongo (mung) beans, available in Asian markets
3 cups water
2 ½ pounds smoked ham hocks (can substitute chicken)
4 cups or more fat-free chicken stock
½ medium onion, diced

1 small ripe tomato, sliced
3 cloves garlic, minced
2 medium Asian eggplants, cut in 2-inch cubes
Salt and pepper to taste

RINSE MONGO BEANS well. In a pot, cook mongo beans in 3 cups water 20 minutes or until soft. If water evaporates, add ⅛ cup water to avoid burning mongo beans.

IN A LARGE POT, bring ham hocks and chicken stock to a boil, then simmer partially covered for 1 hour. Add mongo beans, onion, tomato and garlic, and bring to boil. Add eggplant and cook 5 to 10 minutes. Season with salt and pepper.

Approximate nutrient content per serving, based on ¼ teaspoon total added salt: 260 Calories, 14 grams total fat, 5 grams saturated fat, 65 milligrams cholesterol, 420 milligrams sodium, 11 grams carbohydrate, and 21 grams protein.

🍃 *Low-fat tip: Substitute 2 pounds skinless boneless chicken breast to achieve 1 gram total fat and 140 Calories per serving.*

My classmate Melvin Matsuda is a third-generation Kahuku farmer who grows beautiful eggplant all year-round.

MY FRIEND MUST WAIT

The new Sam Choy's Tokyo restaurant features all the "local flavors" of Hawaiian and Island-style food. Fried poke and laulau are the biggest hits.

We opened the 250-seat restaurant in May 1996 in Daiba, an award-winning city built on Tokyo Bay. There's a beautiful, world-class convention center across from our restaurant — and the city lies right on the shore, which is called Sunset Beach. I was born on the North Shore of O'ahu near a place called Sunset Beach; the coincidence in names made me think we will have good luck with our new restaurant.

Hitoshi Goto bought the franchise for Sam Choy's Tokyo. He and I agreed to bring the Japan chefs out here to Hawai'i for training. The senior chefs and managers come from Hawai'i and the decor was designed by a Hawai'i architect.

I felt it was important to send some of our best people from the Islands to run the place and make sure they stuck to our menu. I take a lot of pride in what I do. It's my name on the building. I thought there might be the chance that if we simply trained the Japanese chefs to cook our way they might revert in a few months or a year or so to making the recipes more local there, and it would evolve into another Japanese restaurant. The point of the

venture is to keep it authentically Hawaiian-style.

I was also concerned about the decor, which we made similar to our Kapahulu place, not the typical Japanese restaurant with square chairs. We have Island-kine chairs, a wood floor, some beautiful artwork by Hawai'i artists. It's a beautiful restaurant, open to the outside in warm weather, and glass doors to slide shut in winter.

If there's a difference over there, it's the Japanese work ethic and manners. I've never walked into a restaurant where the staff all bow at you. Wow. I come back and tell my employees that the Japanese bow and they say, "Uh, bow?" I say, "Yeah, and they say, 'Thank you, thank you for coming and

enjoying your meal here.'" And I tell my people what a nice feeling it is, and how the Japanese instantly make you feel warm and close to them. So I think this opening of the restaurant in Tokyo is a really happy coming together of our two island cultures.

So far it's a huge success. The restaurant is as busy as our O'ahu and Kona restaurants. People line up at the door in Tokyo — Japanese diners, travelers, local people from Hawai'i. The Japanese don't mind waiting outside to get in, but they don't like waiting to be served at a table.

I received a letter from a good friend of mine who's very prominent in Hawai'i. He wrote, "Sam, I figured we would sneak away because we can't get into the Kapahulu restaurant. At the Kona restaurant we can get in, but it's usually a long wait. So we went to Tokyo — and we had to wait two hours!

"I don't know what you do, but I tell you what, when I don't get re-elected to public office, I'll be a partner."

I appreciated his letter. What we're doing is, besides those "local flavors," we're exporting mana. Mana is the Hawaiian word for that energy, those vibes, that feeling of, "Whew, there's electricity in the air." And, the only way you get that feeling is — what you do has to be pure. Pure in the sense that it comes from the heart.

EASY HOLIDAY PORK CHOP AND POTATO SCALLOP

128

MAKES 4 SERVINGS

4 lean pork chops
1 medium onion, julienned
1 can (14 ½ ounces) chicken stock
1 cup milk

½ cup sour cream
2 tablespoons chopped fresh parsley
4 cups thinly sliced unpeeled potatoes
Salt and pepper to taste

This is an easy dish for the busy person. Pop it in the oven, tidy up the house and in 45 minutes open the wrapper to moist pork chops and onion-flavored potatoes.

BROWN PORK CHOPS with onions. Blend chicken stock, milk, sour cream and parsley. In a large casserole dish, alternate layers of potatoes sprinkled with salt and pepper, with layers of sauce. Top with pork chops. Cover and bake in a preheated 350-degree oven for 1 hour, 15 minutes.

Approximate nutrient content per serving, based on no added salt: 390 Calories, 14 grams total fat, 7 grams saturated fat, 85 milligrams cholesterol, 550 milligrams sodium, 38 grams carbohydrate, and 29 grams protein.

Lower-fat tip: In place of milk and sour cream, substitute 1 cup buttermilk mixed with 1 tablespoon cornstarch to achieve 7 grams total fat and 320 Calories per serving.

Sweet Potato Casserole

Makes 12 (1/2-Cup) Servings

6 to 8 medium sweet potatoes
3/4 cup packed brown sugar
1 1/4 cups butter
1 can (1 pound) crushed pineapple
1/2 cup coconut milk

PLACE SWEET POTATOES with their jackets in a steamer basket in 1 1/2 inches of boiling water. Steam covered for 25 minutes or until tender. Peel and cut in 3/8-inch-thick slices. In a buttered casserole dish, layer half EACH of the sweet-potato slices, brown sugar, butter (dot with thin pats) and pineapple. Repeat layers. Pour coconut milk over all. Bake 20 to 25 minutes at 350 degrees.

Approximate nutrient content per serving: 350 Calories, 21 grams total fat, 14 grams saturated fat, 50 milligrams cholesterol, 210 milligrams sodium, 40 grams carbohydrate, and 2 grams protein.

🍃 *Low-fat tip: In place of butter, substitute 1 cup buttermilk mixed with 2 teaspoons cornstarch and 1/2 teaspoon salt to achieve 2.5 grams total fat and 190 Calories per serving.*

My classmate Norman Masuto would give me the real big, off-grade sweet potatoes that his family grew in Kahuku. Top them off with brown sugar and sprinkle nuts on 'em if you want to.

Ka'u Mac Nut-Crusted Roast Loin of Pork with Tropical Marmalade

MAKES 8 SERVINGS

1 boneless pork loin (3 pounds)
1 tablespoon soy sauce
1 tablespoon minced garlic
1/2 teaspoon salt
1/2 teaspoon cracked black pepper
1 1/2 cups Portuguese (or Easter) sweet-bread crumbs
3/4 cup finely chopped macadamia nuts

1/2 cup poha (cape gooseberry) jelly, available in island markets and kitchen-specialty shops
1/2 cup soft butter
1 tablespoon minced parsley
2 teaspoons paprika

Tropical Marmalade, see page 32

Crown a roast pork with rich macadamias grown in the southern Ka'u district of the Big Island. Accompany with a jam-like medley of refreshing island fruits.

PREHEAT OVEN to 350 degrees. Season loin with soy sauce, garlic, salt and black pepper; let stand 20 minutes. Roast for 45 minutes.

MEANWHILE, combine bread crumbs, macadamia nuts, poha jelly, butter, parsley and paprika; mix well. Ten minutes before the end of cooking time, remove roast from oven and coat loin with crumb mixture. Return loin to oven and roast 10 minutes.

LET STAND 10 minutes before carving. Serve with Tropical Marmalade.

Approximate nutrient content per serving pork, based on sirloin pork loin: 650 Calories, 45 grams total fat, 17 grams saturated fat, 155 milligrams cholesterol, 640 milligrams sodium, 25 grams carbohydrate, and 36 grams protein.

Lower-fat tips: Substitute lean top-loin pork; use only 2 tablespoons butter combined with 4 tablespoons buttermilk in crust; and sprinkle a total of 8 teaspoons crushed macadamia nuts over pork, to achieve 15 grams total fat and 400 Calories per serving.

LOCAL BOY SMOKED PORK

132

MAKES 1 SERVING

This combination speaks for itself. Eat it local-style with hot rice. It's a meal in itself. It's the smoked flavor that sends it through (the roof).

1 tablespoon canola oil
6 ounces smoked pork, sliced thin
1 Maui onion, sliced thin
2 tablespoons soy sauce

1 tablespoon brown sugar
1 shot (1 ounce) whiskey
1 cup cooked white rice
1 tablespoon chopped green onion

IN A HEAVY SKILLET, heat oil and brown pork. Add onions and cook 2 minutes or until onions are soft. Add soy sauce, brown sugar and whiskey. (Caution: Do not add whiskey over an open flame because it could ignite.) Cook 2 minutes more. Pour over rice and sprinkle with green onions.

Approximate nutrient content per serving: 780 Calories, 22 grams total fat, 4 grams saturated fat, 95 milligrams cholesterol, at least 1,900 milligrams sodium, 81 grams carbohydrate, and 41 grams protein.

Lower-fat tip: In place of oil, use 4 seconds of nonstick vegetable-oil cooking spray to evenly coat pork and onion before cooking, to achieve 13 grams total fat and 690 Calories per serving.

GRANDMA'S MEATLOAF

MAKES 10 SERVINGS

Meatloaf mixture:
- 1 ½ pounds lean ground beef
- ½ pound ground chicken
- 1 ½ cups toasted bread crumbs
- 1 can (8 ¼ ounces) crushed pineapple, drained well
- ½ cup chopped onion
- ½ cup chopped celery
- 2 eggs
- ¼ cup heavy cream or milk
- ¼ cup soy sauce
- 1 tablespoon minced fresh ginger
- Salt and black pepper to taste
- Chopped green onions

Tailgate Teri Glaze:
- *1 tablespoon cornstarch*
- *2 tablespoons water*
- *1 cup* **Tailgate Teri Sauce,** *see page 111*

My mom makes a good meatloaf. She said, oh, that's Grandma's meatloaf. My grandparents weren't around when I was growing up, so I just have to listen when my mom tells all the stories.

BLEND CORNSTARCH and water to make a smooth paste. In a small saucepan, heat Tailgate Teri Sauce, add cornstarch paste and stir to thicken. Makes 1 cup.

PREHEAT OVEN to 350 degrees. Combine meatloaf-mixture ingredients, blending lightly but well. Press into a loaf pan. Bake 50 minutes. Pour ¼ cup Tailgate Teri Glaze over meatloaf 5 minutes before the end of cooking time.

SLICE MEATLOAF, sprinkle with green onions and serve with remaining ¾ cup Tailgate Teri Glaze.

NOTE: *Meatloaf mixture can be formed into meatballs. Bake meatballs at 350 degrees for 25 to 30 minutes, depending on size. Then, simmer meatballs 5 minutes in Tailgate Teri Glaze. These are excellent as a pupu or an entree.*

Approximate nutrient content per serving meatloaf, based on no salt: 345 Calories, 20 grams total fat, 8 grams saturated fat, 120 milligrams cholesterol, at least 1,000 milligrams sodium, 17 grams carbohydrate, and 21 grams protein.

Lower-fat tip: Substitute 1 pound extra lean ground beef and 1 pound ground chicken, and use milk instead of cream to achieve 14 grams total fat and 290 Calories per serving.

KA MOA
(CHICKEN)

136

Chicken plays a major role in local cooking. It has a delicate texture and a flavor that blends well with many of the ethnic spices. There are just a few handling rules to remember. You never want to freeze, thaw, refreeze, and then use. It's dangerous. Basically, bacteria has an opportunity to grow when you do this. The methods of thawing are also very important. I like to thaw chicken in the refrigerator. But let's be honest — there are times you kind of rush and you bring it out and leave it covered on the counter. Just make sure you heat it to 165 degrees where you're going to kill all the bacteria.

Chicken is a very healthy food if you remove the skin and fat. It's great for moist cooking, like poaching. I like to semi-debone it and make a big pot of chicken stew. It's great on the hibachi. It picks up the grill flavor. I take hibachi-grilled chicken, slice it, and toss it onto a salad. It works well stir-fried with spicy peppers.

People always ask me how I make my roast chicken taste so good. It's all in the basting mixture. I use about 1 tablespoon oil, 1 tablespoon honey, and $1/2$ tablespoon soy sauce, and then baste (or glaze) the meat toward the end of the roasting. Honey is the magic ingredient. It makes it golden brown and gives that sweet taste.

Just remember, like anything else, if you overcook chicken, it becomes like cardboard. So handle with care, it's worth it.

QUICK AND EASY SHOYU CHICKEN

MAKES 6 SERVINGS

1 tablespoon minced cilantro
½ teaspoon Chinese five-spice powder,
   available in supermarkets
2 pounds chicken thighs

1 tablespoon cornstarch
2 tablespoons water
Green onions
Bean sprouts

Tailgate Teri Sauce, *see page 111*

Shoyu chicken, an island classic, features gourmet touches of cilantro, Chinese five spices and fresh-squeezed orange juice.

IN A MEDIUM SAUCEPAN, combine Tailgate Teri Sauce, cilantro and Chinese five-spice powder. Bring to a boil, add chicken, then simmer 20 minutes or until tender. Remove chicken from sauce, set aside and keep warm.

BLEND CORNSTARCH and water to make a smooth paste. Bring 1 cup of sauce to a boil and stir in cornstarch paste to thicken into a glaze. Brush chicken with glaze. Garnish with green onions and bean sprouts.

Approximate nutrient content per serving: 300 Calories, 18 grams total fat, 5 grams saturated fat, 100 milligrams cholesterol, at least 1,000 milligrams sodium, 9 grams carbohydrate, and 23 grams protein.

Lower-fat tip: Use only 1 ½ pounds skinless boneless chicken thighs to achieve 4.5 grams total fat and 190 Calories per serving.

HIBACHI MISO CHICKEN WITH PEANUT BUTTER

MAKES 16 SERVINGS

5 pounds boneless chicken thighs

Marinade:
   *1/2 cup miso (fermented soybean paste),
       available in Asian section of markets*
   1/2 cup smooth peanut butter

1/2 cup soy sauce
1/2 cup sugar
1/2 cup beer
2 tablespoons minced fresh ginger
1 tablespoon minced garlic

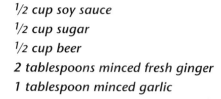

COMBINE MARINADE INGREDIENTS and marinate chicken overnight in refrigerator. Grill over charcoal. There is not enough rice in the world to eat when you start eating this dish!

Approximate nutrient content per serving: 400 Calories, 26 grams total fat, 7 grams saturated fat, 120 milligrams cholesterol, 920 milligrams sodium, 11 grams carbohydrate, and 29 grams protein.

Lower-fat tip: Substitute 5 pounds skinless boneless chicken breast to achieve 6 grams total fat and 250 Calories per serving.

The marinade melds traditional and modern flavors — miso and teriyaki with peanut butter and beer. Kamado grill or cover-grill (Weber enclosed grill) the fillets for 35 minutes, or skewer and grill.

SONOMA RESERVE
TURNING LEAF
SONOMA COUNTY
Chardonnay
1994

Steamed Chicken with Lup Cheong

140

Makes 8 Servings

This delectable steamed-chicken dish offers a combination of sweet Chinese-style sausages, cilantro and slivers of fresh ginger — plus a splash of gin.

2 pounds skinless boneless whole chicken leg meat, cut in medium dice
4 Chinese lup cheong sausages (1.5 ounces each), each cut in 10 diagonal slices
Slivered fresh ginger
Chopped cilantro

Marinade:
2 whole eggs
3 tablespoons soy sauce
3 tablespoons cornstarch
2 tablespoons gin
2 tablespoons sugar
2 tablespoons chopped green onions
1 tablespoon minced garlic
1 teaspoon minced fresh ginger

COMBINE MARINADE ingredients and marinate chicken. Then, place chicken in heat-resistant glass pie plate or steaming bowl and lay lup cheong slices on top. Steam 25 to 30 minutes.

GOES GREAT with lots of ginger and cilantro as condiments.

Approximate nutrient content per serving: 350 Calories, 22 grams total fat, 4.5 grams saturated fat, 150 milligrams cholesterol, 640 milligrams sodium, 10 grams carbohydrate, and 28 grams protein.

Lower-fat tip: Substitute 2 pounds skinless boneless chicken breast and use only 3 ounces lup cheong to achieve 6 grams total fat and 230 Calories per serving.

KAHUKU ROAST CHICKEN

MAKES 10 SERVINGS

1 whole roasting chicken

Green onion-honey marinade:
  1 cup soy sauce
  2 tablespoons honey

2 tablespoons sherry
1- or 1 ¹/2-inch piece fresh ginger, minced
2 stalks green onions, cut in ¹/2-inch lengths
2 cloves garlic, minced

USE CLEAN, damp cloth to wipe chicken well. Then, dry well by using paper towels or by hanging in a cool, airy place 1 to 2 hours.

COMBINE MARINADE ingredients, rub into skin of chicken and marinate 1 to 2 hours, turning occasionally. Drain, reserving marinade.

HEAT OVEN to 350 degrees. Place chicken on a rack in roasting pan with several inches of water (to keep drippings from burning). Roast at 30 minutes per pound or until "tender and browned"— basting with reserved marinade every 15 minutes and turning bird occasionally. Use a cleaver to chop chicken, bones and all, in 2-inch pieces.

Approximate nutrient content per serving: 360 Calories, 23 grams total fat, 7 grams saturated fat, 130 milligrams cholesterol, at least 1,500 milligrams sodium, 4 grams carbohydrate, and 29 grams protein.

🐾 *Low-fat tip: Substitute 3 ¹/2 pounds skinless boneless chicken breast to achieve 2 grams total fat and 210 Calories per serving.*

A roaster is bathed and basted in a green onion-honey marinade, then slow-cooked to tender succulence. Kahuku chickens have a unique taste because of what they are fed.

ISLAND-STYLE BARBECUE CORNISH GAME HENS

142

MAKES 6 SERVINGS

I like barbecuing Cornish game hen. It's quite easy. You don't have to worry about too many ingredients. It is a tasty bird, like squab.

3 Cornish game hens (14 ounces each), butterflied
Chopped green onions

Marinade:
½ cup orange juice
¼ cup olive oil
1 small clove garlic, minced
Salt and pepper to taste

COMBINE MARINADE ingredients and marinate game hens 1 to 2 hours in refrigerator, turning hens several times. Grill, skin side first, basting occasionally with reserved marinade. Turn and repeat until done, in 25 to 30 minutes. Garnish with green onions.

Approximate nutrient content per serving, based on ¼ teaspoon salt: 450 Calories, 30 grams total fat, 7 grams saturated fat, 135 milligrams cholesterol, 570 milligrams sodium, 2 grams carbohydrate, and 42 grams protein.

Lower-fat tip: Substitute skinless Cornish game hens and use only 1 tablespoon olive oil to achieve 11 grams total fat and 270 Calories per serving.

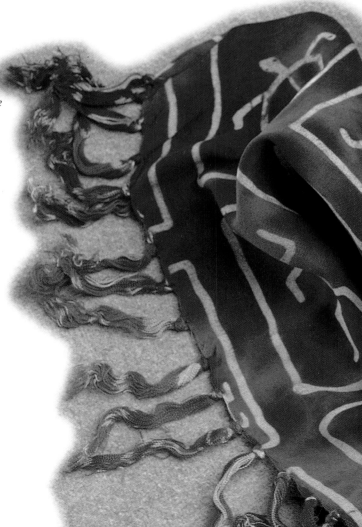

CHICKEN AND PORTUGUESE SAUSAGE KEBABS

144

MAKES 8 SERVINGS

This is an alternative fund-raiser dish. I got the kebab idea as an alternative for those 10 or 15 packages of Portuguese sausage the kids sell to raise funds during baseball season.

1 pound skinless, boneless chicken breast,
**   cut in 1-inch cubes**
1 Portuguese sausage (1 pound),
**   cut in 1-inch chunks**
24 fresh pineapple wedges.

Marinade:
*   1 cup dry red wine*
* $1/2$ cup olive oil*
* $1/4$ cup red wine vinegar*
* $1/4$ cup orange juice*
*   2 tablespoons pineapple juice*
*   3 large cloves garlic, minced*
*   1 tablespoon chopped fresh basil*
*   Salt and cracked peppercorn to taste*

WHISK MARINADE INGREDIENTS together well and marinate chicken cubes 2 or 3 hours. Drain chicken and reserve marinade. On skewers, alternately thread meats and fruit; leave space between chicken and sausage to allow for even cooking. Grill over medium-hot coals 12 minutes or until chicken and sausage are cooked, basting frequently with reserved marinade.

Approximate nutrient content per serving, based on $1/4$ teaspoon total added salt: 440 Calories, 31 grams total fat, 8 grams saturated fat, 75 milligrams cholesterol, 600 milligrams sodium, 14 grams carbohydrate, and 22 grams protein.

Lower-fat tip: Use 1 $1/2$ pounds chicken with $1/2$ pound sausage and only 1 tablespoon olive oil to achieve 11 grams total fat and 270 Calories per serving.

EMU VS. IMU

When we were in Louisiana doing Chef Paul Prudhomme's big festival, we did a lu'au with two kinds of chicken — long rice and shoyu — along with laulau, *squid* lu'au, lomilomi *salmon*, poke, *potato salad,* and a few other standards. But the kalua *pig was the star of the show.*

They charged $150 a person. All the money went to charity. I thought, "Ho, man, this better be a good lu'au."

A guy donated two 200-pound pigs. I said, "Gee, we gotta find a place to kalua *these pigs."*

I got a call from Chris Richard, a big-time lawyer there. "Sam, we're going to cook this pig on the grounds where we're having the lu'au."

It was a huge estate with a big swimming pool, water fountains, colonial pillars and flowers cascading off the pillars, a manicured lawn.

"We're gonna dig an imu on his lawn?" It was like a putting green! But that's exactly what happened. As soon as I started to say, "I don't think so," someone drove a Hop Toad digger out of the garage and they dug the imu right there.

We built the imu and everyone thought imu was the bird — emu. Everybody asked, "Where's the emu? I never tasted an emu." An emu's a flightless bird like an ostrich, and they had one at the estate.

I said, "Well, in Hawai'i, the emu is the imu. We're cooking the food underground."

About 30 people sat around watching as we lit the imu. We smashed the banana stumps (Louisiana has bananas), got the pig into the imu, *threw on ti leaves, banana stumps and leaves, then put burlap bags over everything. The Hop Toad dumped fresh dirt — shhh shhh — and covered the imu all up. I said, "OK, the party's at 7 p.m. Come back at 5 and we'll unveil this imu."

Five o'clock came; the place was packed — 200-something people. Paul Prudhomme was on his electric cart waiting. I started toward the imu, but they gave me a microphone and told me to narrate.

"At 6 o'clock this morning," I said, "we lit the imu and let it burn for two hours until it was real hot. Then, we added the banana stumps." I asked, "Any questions?"

Everybody said, "Wow, an emu. I never tasted an emu before."

I said, "Well, this isn't an E-M-U. It's an I-M-U. The emu is still walking around somewhere."

"See, honey, I told you there was something funny about this Hawaiian emu."

I said, "I need a tester. Who'll be my volunteer?" Three ladies raised their hands. I said, "Try a piece." They pulled apart some meat and ate it. Next thing you know, all the hands were in there.

They went, "This is great," and they were pulling and ripping. It was palahe — *falling off the bone.*

I tell you what, they loved it, they LOVED it. That's the thing about food from Hawai'i. It lights up people's hearts and eyes.

MACADAMIA NUT CHICKEN BREAST WITH TROPICAL MARMALADE

146

MAKES 6 SERVINGS

We encase chicken in a macadamia nut crust. You can't beat it. That keeps all the moisture in for some reason. It's a very popular menu item. It's hot to trot, yeah.

6 skinless, boneless chicken breasts
1 cup finely chopped macadamia nuts
3/4 cup sweet-bread crumbs
1/2 cup flour
3 eggs, lightly beaten
2 tablespoons oil
1 tablespoon butter

Marinade:
1/2 cup soy sauce
1 1/2 tablespoons brown sugar
1 tablespoon mirin (sweet rice wine)
1 tablespoon olive oil
1 teaspoon minced garlic
1 teaspoon minced fresh ginger

***Tropical Marmalade,** see page 20*

COMBINE MARINADE ingredients and marinate chicken 1 hour, turning occasionally. Remove chicken from marinade.

COMBINE MACADAMIA NUTS and sweet-bread crumbs. Dredge chicken in flour, dip in eggs, and coat with macadamia mixture.

IN A HEAVY SKILLET, heat oil and butter on medium heat. Sauté chicken 6 to 7 minutes, turning once. Add a little oil, if necessary, since macadamia nuts may absorb oil. Serve with Tropical Marmalade.

Approximate nutrient content per serving chicken only: 470 Calories, 27 grams total fat, 5 grams saturated fat, 185 milligrams cholesterol, at least 1,400 milligrams sodium, 19 grams carbohydrate, and 36 grams protein.

Lower-fat tips: Consider omitting bread crumbs, flour, eggs, canola oil and butter. Sear meat in a nonstick pan sprayed for 2 seconds with vegetable-oil cooking spray. Use only 1/2 teaspoon olive oil in marinade, and simmer chicken in marinade until done. Top each serving with 1 teaspoon nuts to achieve 4 grams total fat and 190 Calories per serving.

This macadamia nut orchard is located at Mother Goose Farms in Honomalino, south of Kona. John and Vicki Swift raise range-fed sheep in the orchard — that's where I get the Honomalino lamb I like to serve!

CHICKEN BRAISED WITH LILY BUDS AND SHIITAKE MUSHROOMS

MAKES 8 SERVINGS

4 dried shiitake mushrooms

12 dried lily buds, available in Chinese
   markets

1 whole fryer chicken

3 tablespoons canola oil

2 cloves garlic, crushed

3 slices (1/16 inch each) fresh ginger, bruised

1 cup chicken stock

1/2 cup chopped green onions

2 tablespoons chopped cilantro

2 tablespoons sherry

1 tablespoon soy sauce

Shiitake and lily buds add a fragrant earthiness and texture to this slow-cooked dish. Braised chicken suits multi-course family meals, and it reheats easily.

IN SEPARATE SMALL BOWLS of warm water, soak shiitake and lily buds 20 minutes. Cut shiitake in strips. Disjoint chicken and cut in 2-inch pieces.

IN A LARGE, HEAVY PAN, heat oil on medium-high heat. Brown chicken quickly with garlic and ginger. Remove chicken to a plate and set aside.

IN THE SAME PAN, stir together chicken stock, green onions, cilantro, sherry and soy sauce. Return chicken to pan, along with shiitake and lily buds. Bring to a boil; then simmer, covered, 20 minutes or until done.

Approximate nutrient content per serving: 340 Calories, 25 grams total fat, 6 grams saturated fat, 115 milligrams cholesterol, 330 milligrams sodium, 3 grams carbohydrate, and 25 grams protein.

Low-fat tip: Substitute 8 skinless boneless chicken breasts, increase the shiitake to 8, and use only 2 teaspoons canola oil to achieve 3 grams total fat and 170 Calories per serving.

STIR-FRIED CHICKEN OR BEEF FAJITAS

148

MAKES 4 FAJITAS

My (older) son Sam made this recipe up for my friend Tommy Jean Sheldrake's surprise birthday party in California. People loved it. Lucky kid.

1 cup thinly sliced skinless boneless chicken breast (or beef)
1 tablespoon canola oil
4 wheat-flour tortillas
1 cup assorted, sliced fresh vegetables (bell peppers, broccoli, carrots)
1 tablespoon hoisin sauce (sweet-spicy soybean sauce), available in Asian section of supermarkets
Chopped green onions

Marinade:
2 tablespoons soy sauce
1 tablespoon minced fresh ginger
1 tablespoon minced garlic
1 tablespoon chopped green onion
1 teaspoon chopped cilantro
1 teaspoon red chile pepper flakes
1 teaspoon brown sugar
Pinch EACH salt, pepper

COMBINE MARINADE ingredients and marinate meat 15 minutes. In a heavy skillet, heat oil and cook meat about 4 minutes. Add vegetables and cook about 2 minutes more.

IN A DRY SKILLET on high heat, heat tortillas about 30 seconds on each side. On each tortilla, spread 1/4 of the hoisin sauce and top with 1/4 of the meat-vegetable mixture. Sprinkle with green onions and roll up.

Approximate nutrient content per serving, based on 1/16 teaspoon total added salt: 290 Calories, 8 grams total fat, 1 gram saturated fat, 25 milligrams cholesterol, 860 milligrams sodium, 36 grams carbohydrate, and 17 grams protein.

🌶 Low-fat tip: Instead of oil, substitute 5 seconds of nonstick vegetable-oil cooking spray and use low-fat tortillas to achieve 4 grams total fat and 250 Calories per serving.

BREAST OF CHICKEN WITH SHIITAKE SHERRIED BUTTER SAUCE

150

MAKES 6 SERVINGS

Shiitake, sherry and butter enhance chicken breast meat in an elegant ensemble.

6 skinless, boneless chicken breast halves
   (5 ounces each)
Nonstick vegetable-oil cooking spray
Salt and pepper to taste

Shiitake Sherried Butter Sauce:
  2 tablespoons butter
  1 tablespoon chopped onion
  1 clove garlic, minced
  3/4 pound fresh shiitake mushrooms,
    sliced in strips
  1 teaspoon chopped cilantro
  1/2 cup sherry
  1 cup softened butter

SEASON BOTH SIDES of chicken with salt and pepper. Spray nonstick vegetable-oil cooking spray on chicken; then, grill until firm but still moist, turning breasts every 3 or 4 minutes.

TO MAKE SAUCE, in a sauté pan heat the 2 tablespoons butter and sauté onion and garlic until onion is translucent; do not let garlic brown. Add shiitake and cilantro; lightly sauté. Season with salt and pepper. Add sherry to deglaze pan, and simmer until liquid reduces by half. Whisk in the 1 cup butter, a little at a time, until combined well. Adjust seasoning and keep sauce warm until needed. Slice chicken and top with Shiitake Sherried Butter Sauce.

Approximate nutrient content per serving, with 1/4 teaspoon total added salt: 530 Calories, 37 grams total fat, 22 grams saturated fat, 175 milligrams cholesterol, 530 milligrams sodium, 10 grams carbohydrate, and 33 grams protein.

Lower-fat tip: Use only 1/4 cup butter with 1 pound mushrooms and 1 cup sherry to achieve 14 grams total fat and 360 Calories per serving.

UPCOUNTRY SAUSAGE "STUFF IT" CHICKEN   151

MAKES 6 SERVINGS

6 whole chicken-fryer legs (section
 with thigh and drumstick joined)
1 pound Portuguese sausage, casing
 removed
1 cup chopped onion
1/2 cup chopped celery
2 cups Portuguese sweet-bread cubes, toasted

1 cup peeled and diced sweet potato, boiled
 6 to 10 minutes
1/2 cup chopped cilantro
Salt and pepper to taste
1/4 cup honey
2 tablespoons soy sauce

The Portuguese paniolo, or cowboys, of upcountry Maui inspired this dish. Portuguese sausage and Portuguese sweet bread combine in a savory chicken stuffing.

PREHEAT OVEN to 350 degrees. Remove bone from chicken thighs only, by cutting through meat in a straight line along bone. Run thumb and forefinger along bone to separate meat. Cut away bone at end joint. If desired, leave thigh bone attached to drumstick and protruding from meat, as decoration.

IN A SKILLET, sauté sausage; remove to a plate. Sauté onion and celery. Stir in sweet-bread cubes, sweet potato, cilantro, salt, pepper and Portuguese sausage.

DIVIDE STUFFING MIXTURE into 6 portions and press into "deboned" chicken thighs. Place chicken pieces, stuffing side down, in a baking pan and bake 1 hour.

COMBINE HONEY and soy sauce; blend well. During last 15 minutes of baking time, baste chicken several times with honey-soy mixture.

Approximate nutrient content per serving, based on no added salt: 700 Calories, 44 grams total fat, 14 grams saturated fat, 200 milligrams cholesterol, at least 1,350 milligrams sodium, 32 grams carbohydrate, and 44 grams protein.

Lower-fat tip: Use skinless chicken legs and only 1/2 pound sausage to achieve 17 grams total fat and 420 Calories per serving.

Ka I‘a
_____

(Fish)

154

My secrets of fish success are to buy it fresh, don't overcook, and don't let other ingredients dominate. One of the most exciting things about island fish is its freshness. Let me give you a little tip on how to tell how fresh your fish is in the store. Check the color. It should look very bright, like neon pink. For our restaurants, we go to market early in the morning. If possible, you should do the same. Find out when the fish is delivered and buy it as soon as it comes in.

When you're cooking, you want to taste the sweetness of the meat, not the spices or gravy. I like to steam fish fillets. It takes less time. You can put the vegetables in the steaming baskets with the fish. If you're going to use potatoes, then you want to steam them on the bottom, then add the other basket with the fish on top. By the time the potatoes are done, so is your fish. You can carry the steamer right to the table and you've got yourself a healthful, fresh-cooked meal that didn't take more than 10 or 15 minutes. Good idea, eh?

When I work with fish, I try to imagine myself in the fish's environment. I want to make sure not to steal the show, but to let the *'opakapaka* (pink snapper), *moi* (Pacific Threadfin), or *ono* (wahoo) be the main attraction. Use a dainty hand with the seasonings and remember to showcase the fish.

BAKED TERIYAKI MAHIMAHI

MAKES 10 SERVINGS

**4 pounds mahimahi (dolphinfish),
cut in 4-ounce pieces**

Marinade:
  ²/3 cup soy sauce
  6 tablespoons brown sugar
  ¹/4 cup sake

*2 tablespoons orange juice
  or ¹/2 of small orange*
1 tablespoon canola oil
1 ¹/2-inch piece fresh ginger, crushed
1 tablespoon chopped green onions
*1 teaspoon white miso
  (fermented soybean paste)*
2 cloves garlic

*Pair a favorite fish
with a favorite island
preparation style for an
easy, irresistible oven-
baked dish.*

COMBINE MARINADE ingredients and marinate fish 4 to 6 hours in refrigerator.
Arrange mahimahi in a baking dish and bake at 350 degrees 10 to 15 minutes or
until done.

PRESENT ON A PLATTER of shredded cabbage or sautéed fresh vegetables of choice.

Approximate nutrient content per serving: 220 Calories,
2.5 grams total fat, 0.5 gram saturated fat, 130 milligrams
cholesterol, at least 1,100 milligrams sodium, 9 grams
carbohydrate, and 36 grams protein.

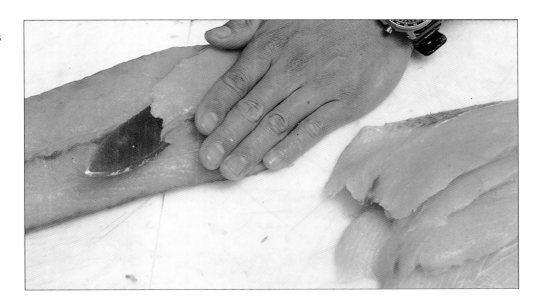

CRUSTED ONO AS FEATURED AT SAM CHOY'S RESTAURANTS

156

MAKES 4 SERVINGS

Crusted ono is one of the bestsellers. It has a kind of reputation, but it works. People love it. It's very good, very good.

4 ono (wahoo) fillets (6 ounces each)
1/4 cup olive oil
1 teaspoon minced fresh ginger
1 teaspoon minced garlic
Salt and pepper to taste
1/2 cup Ritz Cracker crumbs

1/2 cup butter at room temperature
1/4 cup chopped macadamia nuts
1 tablespoon minced fresh herbs
  (combination of basil, dill, thyme)
1 teaspoon paprika

Papaya-Mango Salsa, see page 175

MARINATE ONO for 1 hour in a combination of olive oil, ginger, garlic, salt and pepper.

PREHEAT OVEN to 375 degrees. Combine cracker crumbs, butter, macadamia nuts, herbs and paprika; blend well. Divide cracker-crumb mixture into 4 portions and pat 1 portion on top of each fillet. Bake 8 to 10 minutes.

SERVE WITH Papaya-Mango Salsa.

Approximate nutrient content per serving fish, based on
1/4 teaspoon total added salt: 560 Calories, 45 grams total
fat, 18 grams saturated fat, 125 milligrams cholesterol,
510 milligrams sodium, 5 grams carbohydrate, and
34 grams protein.

*Lower-fat tip: Use only 2 tablespoons each butter and olive oil,
and only 1/4 cup macadamia nuts to achieve 21 grams total
fat and 350 Calories per serving. Or, eat a one-third portion of
this dish as an appetizer.*

LYCHEE OH LYCHEE MONCHONG

MAKES 6 SERVINGS

This dish combines a really oily, moist fish with fruity, flavorful lychees, making for a good marriage.

8 monchong (big-scale pomfret) fillets
    (4 ounces each; see note)
1 tablespoon canola oil
1 tablespoon chicken stock
1/4 cup minced green onion
1 tablespoon minced cilantro
1 1/2 cups canned or fresh lychees,
    shelled and pitted

Marinade:
1/4 cup finely julienned fresh ginger
1 tablespoon sherry
2 teaspoons soy sauce
2 teaspoons cornstarch
1 1/2 teaspoons salt
1 teaspoon sugar

COMBINE MARINADE ingredients and marinate fillets 30 minutes.

IN A WOK, heat oil and fry fillets. Add chicken stock, green onion and cilantro. Cover and simmer 6 to 8 minutes. Remove from heat, add lychees and let stand 5 minutes. Serve with fried rice.

NOTE: *Can substitute mahimahi (dolphinfish), opakapaka (ruby snapper), onaga (red snapper) or salmon.*

Approximate nutrient content per serving fish, based on canned lychees: 220 Calories, 4.5 grams total fat, 0.5 gram saturated fat, 55 milligrams cholesterol, 740 milligrams sodium, 10 grams carbohydrate, and 32 grams protein.

Fresh lychee.

Sautéed Opakapaka with Spinach Coconut Lu'au Sauce

Makes 4 Servings

4 opakapaka (pink snapper) fillets
   (6 ounces each)
1 teaspoon minced fresh ginger
1 teaspoon minced garlic
1/2 teaspoon salt

1/4 teaspoon white pepper
1/4 cup flour
2 tablespoons butter
1 tablespoon olive oil
Spinach Coconut Lu'au Sauce, *see below*

Here's a takeoff on squid lu'au. Take out the squid from that recipe, make a thinner sauce and add it to opakapaka, an excellent flaky fish. The combination is just right — really, really 'ono.

SEASON OPAKAPAKA fillets with ginger, garlic, salt and pepper. Dredge in flour. In a large heavy skillet, heat butter and oil. Sauté fish just until cooked; do not overcook.

TRANSFER FISH to a warm serving platter and serve with Spinach Coconut Lu'au Sauce.

Approximate nutrient content per serving fish only:
280 Calories, 11 grams total fat, 4.5 grams saturated fat,
80 milligrams cholesterol, 430 milligrams sodium,
6 grams carbohydrate, and 36 grams protein.

Lower-fat tip: Sauté fish in only 2 teaspoons butter and 1 teaspoon olive oil in a nonstick frying pan to achieve 5 grams total fat and 230 Calories per serving.

Spinach Coconut Lu'au Sauce

Makes 10 (1-Ounce) Servings

3 tablespoons minced Maui onion
1/2 teaspoon minced fresh ginger
2 tablespoons butter
1 cup heavy cream
1/4 cup coconut milk
Salt, pepper and sugar to taste

1/2 cup cooked fresh lu'au
   (young taro leaves; chopped fresh
   spinach can be used as a substitute)

Cooking fresh lu'au, see page 118

Approximate nutrient content per 1-ounce serving, based on total addition of 1/4 teaspoon salt and 1 teaspoon sugar: 120 Calories, 12 grams total fat, 8 grams saturated fat, 40 milligrams cholesterol, 85 milligrams sodium, 2 grams carbohydrate, and 1 gram protein.

Lower-fat tip: Substitute half-and-half and low-fat coconut milk, such as Globe or Trader Joe's (1 gram fat per tablespoon), and use only 1 tablespoon butter to achieve 4.5 grams total fat and 50 Calories per serving.

IN A SMALL SAUCEPAN, sauté onions and ginger in butter 3 minutes or until onions are translucent. Add heavy cream, bring to a boil and reduce by half. Stir in cooked lu'au (or spinach) and coconut milk, and cook 2 minutes. Season to taste with salt, pepper, and sugar.

BAKED WHOLE OPAKAPAKA WITH COCONUT MILK

MAKES 10 SERVINGS

6 ti leaves (can use banana leaves,
   corn husks or aluminum foil)
3-pound whole opakapaka
   (pink snapper) or fillets
1 ½ tablespoons Hawaiian (sea) salt

1 tablespoon minced fresh ginger
½ cup mayonnaise
Aluminum foil
1 ½ cups coconut milk
1 Maui onion, diced

I remember doing this on my TV cooking show. Ho, the people called me on that recipe. It was the bes' they ever had. It was really good, really ono, really everything.

RINSE TI LEAVES and strip the back of the leaf-ribs so leaves become flexible.

SCALE, CLEAN and score whole opakapaka. Sprinkle Hawaiian salt and ginger on fish and spread mayonnaise over its surface. Place fish on ti leaves arranged on a large piece of foil. Pour coconut milk and sprinkle onions over fish. Wrap fish in ti leaves, then seal in foil. Bake at 350 degrees 25 to 30 minutes, depending on thickness of fish.

Approximate nutrient content per serving: 360 Calories, 22 grams total fat, 10 grams saturated fat, 70 milligrams cholesterol, 1,400 milligrams sodium, 3 grams carbohydrate, and 36 grams protein.

Lower-fat tip: Substitute nonfat mayonnaise and use low-fat coconut milk, such as Globe or Trader Joe's (1 gram fat per tablespoon) to achieve 5 grams total fat and 215 Calories per serving.

MONCHONG WITH ONION COMPOTE

162

MAKES 4 SERVINGS

Monchong is a different, oily breed of fish that's just coming on. A sweet onion compote works great on that monchong: It's like having steak and onions.

5 tablespoons unsalted butter
3 Maui onions, minced
1/2 cup minced green onion
1 teaspoon minced fresh ginger
3 tablespoons brandy, such as E & J VSOP (very special old pale) brandy
1 cup heavy cream

Salt and pepper to taste
4 monchong (big-scale pomfret) fillets (5 ounces each)
2 cups fish stock, clam juice or chicken stock
2 tablespoons olive oil
Flour

TO PREPARE ONION COMPOTE: In a large, heavy skillet, melt 3 tablespoons of the butter on low heat. Add onions, green onions and ginger. Cover and cook, stirring occasionally, 15 minutes or until tender. Add brandy and 1/3 cup of the cream. Cover and cook, stirring occasionally, 5 minutes or until onions are very tender. Season with salt and pepper.

TO PREPARE SAUCE: In medium-size heavy saucepan, boil fish stock and remaining 2/3 cup heavy cream, stirring occasionally, 20 minutes or until reduced to sauce consistency. Season with salt and pepper.

TO PREPARE FISH: Season fillets with salt and pepper, and dredge in flour. In another large heavy skillet, melt remaining 2 tablespoons butter and olive oil on medium-high heat. Cook fillets 3 or 4 minutes per side or until just done.

ON INDIVIDUAL PLATES, arrange fillets, top with onion compote and ladle sauce over all.

Approximate nutrient content per serving, based on no added salt: 600 Calories, 45 grams total fat, 24 grams saturated fat, 175 milligrams cholesterol, 380 milligrams sodium, 10 grams carbohydrate, and 32 grams protein.

Lower-fat tip: Substitute half-and-half for cream, and use only 1 tablespoon butter to sauté onions, and 1 tablespoon each butter and olive oil to sauté fish, to achieve 18 grams total fat and 360 Calories per serving.

TSUKIJI FISH MARKET

I f you want to see seafood, then Tokyo's Tsukiji Fish Market is the place to drop anchor.

This is the world's largest fish market. It's so huge and so packed with bluefin tuna, that on any predawn morning when the fish auctioneer's bell rings, the bluefins are lined up like so many sardines canned in an airplane hangar.

Tsukiji's auction is big, I mean really BIG. Once the sale starts, the fishmongers create an uproar by screaming their prices to buyers, who order their fresh fish by hand gestures.

Each year Japanese fishermen catch more than 12 million tons of fish, supplemented by another 2 million pounds of imported marine products. Japan leads the world in fishing with some 400,000 fishing vessels plying the ocean.

Besides the enormous bluefin catches, Tsukiji offers hundreds of kinds of seafood. It's amazing. There are flatfish, mackerel, pollock, sardines, clams, oysters, scallops, crabs, shrimp, eels, octopus, squid, and edible seaweed.

The Japanese eat almost a million tons of tuna every year, mainly as sashimi, that raw fish delicacy. They prize the cold-water, high-fat Atlantic bluefins. The lower-fat bluefin tuna from Hawai'i's warm waters makes only the second team on the Japan fish market—usually in the summertime when it's very cheap.

Fishermen from Nantucket and Cape Cod, Massachusetts, flash freeze the whole Atlantic bluefin tunas inside thick casings of ice. After the bluefins reach Tsukiji Fish Market and are auctioned off, band saws cut through the ice casings and quarter the fish. Then, fish handlers use huge knives to chop off the bony parts and carve the prime fillet into sashimi blocks. They wrap up these blocks and they sell them.

I was always taught to cut sashimi in a certain way, but in Tokyo they cut the semifrozen fish like steaks. They leave the cut fish in blocks and place them in holding pans.

When you go into a Tokyo sashimi bar, the chef peels the sashimi slices off like a deck of cards; the pieces are perfectly uniform in size and shape. The iciness has just melted, so the sashimi is frosty cold and tastes very sweet.

I compare that industrial-strength fish scene at Tsukiji Market to the kind of down-home backyard fishing I've done in Hawaiian waters, and I kind of feel like I've seen both ends of the spectrum. Sometimes I'll go out with my friends into the waters off the Kona coast to catch weke'ula, which is a red bottom fish of the goatfish family that swims between 20 to 35 fathoms (six feet to a fathom). It's mostly caught with an outrigger. We found the best method is not to use bait because that attracts too many other kinds of fishes. So we use yarn. That's right, yarn, all those different colored kinds, which we wrap around a hook so that when it's in the water it opens up like a squid. We tie four or five hooks on the line, and trolling through a school we can catch as many as we have hooks.

What you do is let your line sink to the bottom. When you feel it hit, you bounce your pole so the little yarn squids dance for the fish. You feel a fish bite, and then another one, and another. Pretty soon your pole will start getting real heavy, and you just crank it up. The fish fight each other, one pulling this way, the other that, and they're helping you pull them upward. You end up with all these fish, and they're very good, very tasty.

Frozen bluefins on the Tsukiji auction block.

SEARED NIHOA OPAH

164

MAKES 2 SERVINGS

Long-line fishermen catch opah (moonfish) 100 pounds and larger off Nihoa islet at the northern tip of the Hawaiian Islands. This dish's layered presentation makes it more exciting.

2 tablespoons canola oil
4 opah (moonfish) fillets (3 ounces each)
¼ cup julienned carrots and zucchini
4 fresh shiitake mushrooms, sliced
1 tablespoon soy sauce
1 tablespoon oyster sauce

Marinade:
1 tablespoon minced fresh ginger
1 tablespoon minced garlic
1 tablespoon chopped cilantro
1 tablespoon brown sugar
Pinch EACH salt, pepper

COMBINE MARINADE ingredients and marinate fish 5 minutes.

IN A HEAVY SKILLET, heat oil and cook fillets about 2 minutes on each side. Transfer fish to a warm plate. Add carrots and zucchini to skillet and cook about 2 minutes.

ON A PLATE, arrange 2 opah fillets and top with carrots and zucchini. Place remaining 2 opah fillets on top. To the skillet add mushrooms, soy sauce and oyster sauce. Cook mixture about 2 minutes, then pour over fish.

Approximate nutrient content per serving, based on ¹⁄₁₆ teaspoon total added salt: 390 Calories, 21 grams total fat, 3 grams saturated fat, 65 milligrams cholesterol, at least 1,000 milligrams sodium, 13 grams carbohydrate, and 37 grams protein.

Lower-fat tip: Spray fish and vegetables with nonstick vegetable-oil cooking spray instead of using canola oil to fry, to achieve 12 grams total fat and 310 Calories per serving.

Opah Macadamia Nori with Dill Cream Sauce

Makes 4 Servings

Be creative using Japanese nori — not only with sushi, but hey, wrap fish with it. It's natural seaweed from the ocean and when you cook it, it becomes crispy.

8 opah (moonfish) fillets (3 ounces each)
1/4 cup olive oil
1 tablespoon minced fresh herbs
   (combination of basil, dill,
   thyme and/or rosemary)
Salt and black pepper to taste
Flour

3 eggs, beaten
1 cup finely chopped macadamia nuts
4 sheets nori (seasoned dried seaweed
   used for sushi)
2 tablespoons canola oil

Dill Cream Sauce, see page 175

MARINATE FISH 1 hour in a combination of olive oil, fresh herbs, salt and pepper. Dust marinated fillets with flour, and dip in egg wash and then dip in macadamia nuts. Cut nori into 8 strips, each 1 by 4 inches. Wrap 1 nori strip around top of each fillet.

IN A SKILLET, heat oil and sauté wrapped fillets until golden brown. On individual plates, lace Dill Cream Sauce and top with Opah Macadamia Nori fillets.

Approximate nutrient content per serving fish only:
660 Calories, 52 grams total fat, 9 grams saturated fat,
230 milligrams cholesterol, 340 milligrams sodium,
8 grams carbohydrate, and 41 grams protein.

Lower-fat tip: Omit flour and eggs; use only 1 tablespoon olive oil and 2 teaspoons canola oil; and sprinkle a total of 6 tablespoons macadamia nuts over dish, to achieve 15 grams total fat and 280 Calories per serving.

BLACKENED EHU WITH TROPICAL SALSA

MAKES 2 SERVINGS

2 tablespoons soy sauce
2 tablespoons honey
1 (8-ounce) fillet of ehu (orange snapper)
   or other preferred fish
2 tablespoons canola oil

Tropical Salsa, *see below*

Blackening mix:
   1 tablespoon paprika
   1 tablespoon cayenne
   1 teaspoon ground pepper
   1 teaspoon garlic salt
   1 teaspoon salt
   1 teaspoon powdered oregano
   1 teaspoon dried crumbled thyme

What excites me is blackening snapper, with the inside just cooked. When you fork it, you can see the juices literally running out. Make sure the salsa is really fresh.

COMBINE BLACKENING-MIX ingredients and set aside.

MIX SOY SAUCE and honey, and coat fish with mixture. Roll fish in blackening mix.

IN A HEAVY SKILLET, heat oil until it starts to smoke. Lower fish carefully into oil to prevent splashing hot oil. Cook about 3 minutes on each side, depending on thickness of fish. Serve with Tropical Salsa.

Approximate nutrient content per serving fish only: 410 Calories, 17 grams total fat, 1.5 grams saturated fat, 40 milligrams cholesterol, at least 2,500 milligrams sodium, 41 grams carbohydrate, and 27 grams protein.

Lower-fat tip: Use only 2 teaspoons canola oil to achieve 7 grams total fat and 330 Calories per serving.

TROPICAL SALSA 🍃

MAKES 8 (¼ CUP) SERVINGS

½ cup diced fresh mango
½ cup diced fresh papaya
½ cup diced fresh pineapple
¼ cup diced red bell pepper

2 tablespoons chopped cilantro
1 teaspoon sugar
1 teaspoon vinegar

Approximate nutrient content per ¼-cup serving: 20 Calories, no fat, no saturated fat, no cholesterol, no sodium, 5 grams carbohydrate, and no protein.

COMBINE INGREDIENTS and refrigerate until served.

STUFFED 'AHI WITH HANA BUTTER AND PAPAYA COULIS

MAKES 4 SERVINGS

4 'ahi (yellowfin tuna) fillets
    (6 ounces each; see note)

Flour

2 egg whites, lightly beaten

3/4 cup sesame seeds, toasted in dry skillet

2 tablespoons canola oil

Hana Butter and Papaya Coulis,
    see page 170

This is like chicken Kiev, with seasoned butter inside a big chunk of 'ahi tuna. Bake it or deep-fry it. What's good is when you cut it open, the butter just oozes out.

FOR EACH SERVING, roll a fish fillet around a one-fourth section of Hana Butter log. Coat the rolled fillet with flour, dip in egg white and coat with sesame seeds.

IN A SKILLET, heat oil on medium heat and sauté fish until lightly browned. Place fillets on a baking sheet and bake 5 to 6 minutes in a 350-degree preheated oven.

SPOON PAPAYA COULIS onto individual plates and top with fillets.

NOTE: *Substitute a firm fish, such as swordfish (shutome), ono (wahoo), other tuna (aku, tombo) or marlin (kajiki, nairagi).*

Approximate nutrient content per serving with coulis, based on 1/4 teaspoon total added salt in Hana Butter: 580 Calories, 33 grams total fat, 10 grams saturated fat, 110 milligrams cholesterol, 350 milligrams sodium, 27 grams carbohydrate, and 47 grams protein.

Lower-fat tip: Use only 1/4 cup sesame seeds, 1 tablespoon canola oil and one-half of the Hana Butter to achieve 15 grams total fat and 400 Calories per serving.

PAPAYA COULIS 🦋

170

MAKES 4 (½-CUP) SERVINGS

1 ripe papaya, seeded and peeled
    (see note)
1 tablespoon white vinegar

1 tablespoon sugar
¼ cup finely chopped cilantro

DICE ENOUGH PAPAYA to make ½cup.

MACHINE PROCESS remaining papaya to make a purée. In a small saucepan, combine papaya purée, vinegar and sugar; cook 5 minutes. Stir in diced papaya and cilantro.

NOTE: *Can substitute other fresh fruits, such as mango, pineapple, nectarine, peach or plum.*

Approximate nutrient content per serving: 50 Calories, no fat, no cholesterol, no sodium, 14 grams carbohydrate, and no protein.

"DA HANA BUTTER"

MAKES ¼ CUP (1 LOG)

¼ cup softened butter
1 tablespoon minced cilantro
Salt and coarsely ground black
    pepper to taste
Pinch red chile pepper flakes

BLEND ALL INGREDIENTS and shape into a log, ½ inch in diameter. Freeze until firm. Cut into 4 sections.

PAN-FRIED CATFISH WITH SAM'S SWEET & SOUR SAUCE

MAKES 2 SERVINGS

2 catfish fillets, 4 ounces each

Pinch EACH salt, pepper

Flour

2 tablespoons canola oil

1 tablespoon minced fresh ginger

1 tablespoon minced garlic

1 cup assorted sliced vegetables, such as
    bell peppers, tomatoes, carrots, onion
    and broccoli florets

1 tablespoon prepared hot mustard

1 tablespoon chopped green onion

1/2 cup bottled Sam Choy's Kona Cuisine
    Island Style Sweet & Sour Sauce or
    3/4 cup Sweet & Sour Sauce

Sweet & Sour Sauce:

Makes 1 1/2 cups

1 cup sugar

1/2 cup tomato ketchup

1/2 cup vinegar

1/2 cup water

1/4 cup orange marmalade

2 tablespoons pineapple juice

2 teaspoons soy sauce

1 1/2 teaspoons minced ginger

1 teaspoon minced garlic

1/4 teaspoon hot pepper sauce

*2 tablespoons cornstarch blended
    with 1 1/2 tablespoons water*

This recipe is dedicated to those people who are starting to raise catfish in Wai'anae, Waimanalo, Waimea on the Big Island, and up in Hilo side.

SEASON FILLETS with salt and pepper, then dust with flour. Heat oil in a frying pan over medium-high heat, and cook fish about 3 minutes on each side. Remove fish to a warm platter.

ADD GINGER, garlic and vegetables to frying pan and cook about 2 minutes. Add Sweet & Sour Sauce and mustard; cook stirring for 1 minute or until mixture is heated through. Pour sweet & sour mixture over fish.

SWEET & SOUR SAUCE: Blend cornstarch and 1 1/2 tablespoons water to form a paste; set aside. In a saucepan, combine remaining ingredients. Bring to a boil and add cornstarch paste. Reduce heat and simmer, stirring frequently, until thickened.

Approximate nutrient content per serving, based on 1/16 teaspoon total added salt: 400 Calories, 27 grams total fat, 3 grams saturated fat, 55 milligrams cholesterol, 290 milligrams sodium, 29 grams carbohydrate, and 20 grams protein.

Lower-fat tip: Use only 1 teaspoon canola oil in a nonstick frying pan to fry fish (without flour coating), and spray vegetables with nonstick vegetable-oil cooking spray before stir-frying, to achieve 15 grams total fat and 270 Calories per serving.

Approximate nutrient content per 2-tablespoon Sweet & Sour Sauce serving: 50 Calories, no fat, no cholesterol, 90 milligrams sodium, 13 grams carbohydrate and no protein.

POACHED UKU WITH HOLLANDAISE AND POHA BERRY SAUCE

172

MAKES 6 SERVINGS

Poaching fish is good — it's healthful and it allows you to have control over the moisture in the cooked fish. It adds juices because you are poaching in seasoned water.

6 fillets (6 ounces each) of uku (gray snapper) or other white fish

Poaching water:
4 cups water
1 cup chardonnay or other dry white wine
¹/₄ cup chopped onion

¹/₄ cup chopped carrot
¹/₄ cup chopped celery
4 sprigs cilantro
¹/₈ teaspoon thyme

Hollandaise Sauce and Poha Berry Sauce, *see opposite page*

IN A STOCKPOT, combine poaching-water ingredients. Bring to a boil, then simmer 30 minutes. Do not stir. Skim off foam.

MEANWHILE, prepare Hollandaise Sauce and Poha Berry Sauce.

THEN, POACH UKU FILLETS in poaching water 10 minutes or until just done. Serve topped with Hollandaise. Drizzle Poha Berry Sauce over all in a decorative pattern. Approximate preparation time: 1 hour.

THIS DISH goes great with boiled potatoes.

The sought-after poha berry and poha jam.

Approximate nutrient content per serving, based on 2 tablespoons hollandaise and 1 tablespoon poha sauce: 390 Calories, 25 grams total fat, 15 grams saturated fat, 160 milligrams cholesterol, 420 milligrams sodium, 3 grams carbohydrate, and 36 grams protein.

Lower-fat tip: Use lower-fat hollandaise sauce (see its lower-fat tip) and double the poha sauce to achieve 11 grams total fat and 280 Calories per serving.

HOLLANDAISE SAUCE

MAKES 1 ½ CUPS SERVINGS

¼ cup dry white wine
Juice of 1 lemon
1 teaspoon salt

Pinch EACH white pepper, cayenne
4 egg yolks
3 cups clarified butter

IN A SAUCEPAN, boil wine, lemon juice, salt and white and cayenne peppers until reduced by half. Remove pan from heat and cool for a few minutes.

WITH A WIRE WHISK, beat wine mixture constantly while doing the following: Add egg yolks one at a time. Reheat mixture on very low heat (or place over a pan of very hot water, double-boiler style). When creamy, remove from heat and cool (beating gently) until sauce is barely cool enough to touch. Then, add a few drops clarified butter. Continue whisking in butter very gradually until fully incorporated.

IF SAUCE THICKENS, whisk in a little warm water at a time.

Approximate nutrient content per 2-tablespoon serving: 210 Calories, 23 grams total fat, 14 grams saturated fat, 95 milligrams cholesterol, 310 milligrams sodium, no carbohydrate, and 1 gram protein.

Lower-fat tip: Substitute 1 cup white sauce and, while simmering, whisk in, in order, 4 beaten egg yolks, 6 tablespoons butter and 1 tablespoon lemon juice, to achieve 9 grams total fat and 90 Calories per serving.

POHA BERRY SAUCE 🦐

MAKES 1 ½ CUPS

2 cups fresh poha berries (cape goose-
      berries) or other gooseberries
3 tablespoons sugar

2 tablespoons water
Juice from 1 medium orange

MACHINE PROCESS poha berries to form a purée. In a small saucepan, bring poha purée, sugar and water to boil. Add orange juice to taste.

Approximate nutrient content per 1-tablespoon serving: 10 Calories, no fat, no cholesterol, no sodium, 3 grams carbohydrate, and no protein.

CRISPY FISH WITH SAM CHOY'S BOTTLED ISLAND-STYLE SWEET & SOUR SAUCE

174

MAKES 8 SERVINGS

Deep-frying adds a crispy crust to fish and the moisture inside is great, too. The sweet & sour sauce takes it to another level: It's not fat on fat, but fat on zero fat.

2 ½ pounds ono (wahoo),
    cut in 3-ounce fillets
1 egg
1 tablespoon water
¼ cup flour
¼ cup cornstarch
Vegetable oil for deep-frying, such as
    safflower, cottonseed or corn oil
1 bottle (12 ounces) Sam Choy's Kona
    Cuisine Island-Style Sweet & Sour Sauce
    or ¾ cup Sweet & Sour Sauce
See Sweet & Sour Sauce, page 171

Marinade:
    1 tablespoon soy sauce
    1 tablespoon canola oil
    1 teaspoon minced fresh ginger
    Salt and pepper to taste

COMBINE MARINADE ingredients and marinate fish 30 mintues.

BEAT TOGETHER egg and water. Combine flour and cornstarch. Dip marinated fillets in egg wash, then in flour mixture to coat. In a wok, heat oil and deep-fry until golden brown. Drain on absorbent paper.

NOW, HERE'S THE HARD PART: Open bottle of Sam Choy's Kona Cuisine Island Style Sweet & Sour Sauce. Pour sauce, at room temperature or warmed, over crispy fish. Now, how hard can that be?

Approximate nutrient content per serving, based on ¹/₁₆ teaspoon total added salt: 500 Calories, 37 grams total fat, 5 grams saturated fat, 95 milligrams cholesterol, 310 milligrams sodium, 19 grams carbohydrate, and 30 grams protein.

Lower-fat tip: Use only 1 teaspoon canola oil in a nonstick pan to sauté fish (without flour coating) instead of deep-frying, then finish cooking fish in sweet & sour sauce to achieve 15 grams total fat and 275 Calories per serving.

GOSSAMER BAY
V I N E Y A R D S
WASHINGTON STATE
SAUVIGNON BLANC
1993

Papaya-Mango Salsa 🦋

Makes 2 ½ Cups

3 tablespoons sugar
1 ½ tablespoons vinegar
Pinch red chile pepper flakes
Pinch cumin
1 medium papaya, seeded,
   peeled and diced

1 cup peeled and diced mango
½ small red onion, diced
3 tablespoons diced red bell pepper
2 tablespoons chopped cilantro

Mix sugar, vinegar, chile flakes and cumin until sugar dissolves. Fold in remaining ingredients.

Approximate nutrient content per 2-tablespoon serving: 20 Calories, no fat, no cholesterol, no sodium, 5 grams carbohydrate, and no protein.

Dill Cream Sauce

Makes About 1 Cup, or 8 (2-Tablespoon) Servings

1 tablespoon minced shallots
1 tablespoon butter
½ cup white wine
2 cups heavy cream

1 tablespoon minced fresh dill
   (or ½ teaspoon dried dill leaves)
Salt and pepper to taste

In a small saucepan, sauté shallots in butter and wine 8 minutes. Add cream, bring to a boil and reduce by half. Stir in dill and season with salt and pepper.

Approximate nutrient content per 2-tablespoon serving, based on ¼ teaspoon total added salt: 230 Calories, 24 grams total fat, 15 grams saturated fat, 85 milligrams cholesterol, 105 milligrams sodium, 2 grams carbohydrate, and 1 gram protein.

🦋 *Low-fat tip: Substitute 1 ¼ cups buttermilk and 1 ¼ cups nonfat yogurt in place of cream and wine, and use only 1 teaspoon butter to achieve 1 gram total fat and 40 Calories per serving.*

KA IʻA PŪPŪ

(SHELLFISH)

178

You can use just about any cooking style when you're working with shellfish. Their flavors blend well in stir-fry, cioppino, au gratin, or curry with coconut milk. They can be poached, grilled, baked, or steamed. Their versatility is astonishing. They're also good in combinations: shrimp and clams, lobster and crab, oysters and abalone.

I have to say that shrimp are my favorite. I like them poached in water seasoned with lemon, onion, carrot, celery, and a little fresh dill.

Shrimp tend to be a little rubbery if they're not cooked right. There are two secrets to getting a perfect shrimp cocktail — one is don't overcook, and the other is keep the shrimp moist.

I have this method of cooking shrimp that works every time. Combine the ingredients to season the poaching "brine" and bring it to a boil. Remove the seasonings and drop the shrimp in the boiling liquid. The rolling bubbles will calm a bit but, as soon as you see them return, the shrimp is cooked just right — perfect, nice and sweet. Remove the pot from the heat to let the poaching water cool slightly. Scoop out the shrimp and chill them. When the shrimp are cold, put them back in the brine, and let the two sit in the refrigerator until you're ready to eat. The shrimp are so moist when they're prepared this way, perfect for shrimp cocktail. Add some garlic to a cocktail sauce and you're set for a shellfish treat.

I demonstrated how to poach shrimp in a huge wok at Kapi'olani Community College.

Shrimp Curry with Coconut Milk and Sugar Snap Peas

179

Makes 6 Servings (Pictured on pages 176/177)

1 pound extra-large shrimp (about 16
    to 20), peeled and deveined
6 tablespoons butter
2 tablespoons olive oil
1 small onion, finely chopped
1 tablespoon curry powder
1 teaspoon sugar
1/2 teaspoon minced fresh ginger

1/2 teaspoon salt
Pepper to taste
1/4 cup flour
2 cups heavy cream
1 cup chicken stock
1/2 cup coconut milk
2 cups blanched fresh sugar snap peas

This is my kids' favorite. My wife cooks it, I cook it, the kids love it. I think a lot of other people also love it. The secret is don't overcook the shrimp.

In a heavy skillet, heat 2 tablespoons of the butter and olive oil, and sauté onion and curry powder until onion is translucent. Add shrimp, sugar, ginger, salt and pepper. Sauté 3 or 4 minutes, then remove to a plate.

In the skillet, melt remaining 4 tablespoons butter, stir in flour and cook 5 minutes. Slowly add cream, chicken stock and coconut milk, stirring constantly until mixture is smooth and thick. Return shrimp to pan, along with snap peas; heat through. Serve with steamed rice.

Cooking Tip:

Allow yourself to make fresh coconut milk. It's definitely a winner. The process is not hard with the juicers available today.

Buy already husked coconuts in the markets. Use a hammer to crack a husked coconut. Take a butter knife to dig out the coconut meat. Cut the coconut meat into small strips. Drop the coconut strips into a juicer and extract the milk. Strain the coconut milk through cheesecloth. Dilute the thick and rich coconut milk by adding 1/2 cup water to 1 cup fresh coconut milk; then add to a favorite recipe.

Approximate nutrient content per serving: 550 Calories,
51 grams total fat, 30 grams saturated fat, 230 milligrams
cholesterol, 600 milligrams sodium, 13 grams carbohydrate,
and 14 grams protein.

*Lower-fat tip: Substitute half-and-half in place of cream;
use low-fat coconut milk, such as Globe or Trader Joe's
(1 tablespoon fat per tablespoon); and use only 1 tablespoon
each butter and olive oil, to achieve 16 grams total fat
and 260 Calories per serving.*

STIR-FRIED U-10 SHRIMPS AND FRESH ASPARAGUS

MAKES 4 SERVINGS

1 pound fresh asparagus

1 tablespoon salted fermented black beans,
  soaked in water and drained

2 tablespoons minced green onion

1 garlic clove, minced

1/2 teaspoon minced fresh ginger

1 tablespoon soy sauce

1/2 teaspoon sesame seed oil

1/2 teaspoon brown sugar

2 teaspoons cornstarch

2 teaspoons cold water

1 tablespoon canola oil

12 peeled and deveined U-10 shrimps
  ("Under 10" per pound)

1/2 cup chicken stock

Besides shiitake mushrooms, asparagus lights up a lot of people. So I call this my 1-2 punch, shrimp being at the top of the list, with asparagus right after. It's a winner.

TRIM TOUGH WHITE ENDS from asparagus and cut stalks in 1/2-inch diagonal slices. Mash black beans with green onions, garlic and ginger; stir in soy sauce, sesame oil and sugar. Mix cornstarch and cold water to form a paste; set aside.

IN A WOK, heat 2 teaspoons of the oil and stir-fry shrimp 2 minutes or until it turns pink; remove to a plate. Heat remaining 1 teaspoon oil and stir-fry asparagus. Stir in black-bean mixture and shrimp. Add stock and heat quickly. Stir in cornstarch paste, a little at a time, to thicken. Serve over steamed rice or noodles.

Approximate nutrient content per serving:
  160 Calories, 6 grams total fat, 1 gram saturated fat,
  160 milligrams cholesterol, 680 milligrams sodium,
  8 grams carbohydrate, and 21 grams protein.

BAKED SCALLOPS AU GRATIN WITH FRESH ASPARAGUS

182

MAKES 6 SERVINGS

This recipe gives you the feeling of being creative, yet it's simple. Set it all up in your dish, sprinkle the top with Parmesan, pop it in the oven and it's done.

1 ½ pounds scallops
1 cup dry white wine
¼ cup chopped green onion
1 tablespoon chopped fresh dill
½ teaspoon salt
4 tablespoons butter

2 tablespoons flour
½ cup heavy cream
Salt and white pepper to taste
24 fresh asparagus, trimmed and blanched
1 tablespoon bread crumbs
¼ cup freshly grated Parmesan cheese

CUT SCALLOPS IN HALF, depending on size.

IN A MEDIUM SAUCEPAN, simmer together wine, green onions, dill and salt 2 or 3 minutes. Add scallops and simmer covered for 1 ½ to 2 minutes; remove scallops to a bowl. Boil wine mixture until reduced to ½ cup liquid.

IN A SAUCEPAN, cook 2 tablespoons of the butter with flour for 2 minutes. Stir in hot wine reduction and cream. Adjust seasoning with salt and white pepper. Stir in scallops.

IN 4 SMALL CASSEROLE DISHES, layer, in order: asparagus, scallops, bread crumbs and Parmesan. Melt remaining 2 tablespoons butter and drizzle over mini-casseroles. Broil casseroles until bubbling hot and lightly browned. Serve immediately.

Approximate nutrient content per serving, based on ½ teaspoon total added salt: 310 Calories, 17 grams total fat, 10 grams saturated fat, 90 milligrams cholesterol, 530 milligrams sodium, 9 grams carbohydrate, and 23 grams protein.

Lower-fat tip: Substitute ½ cup buttermilk mixed with 1 teaspoon cornstarch in place of cream, and use only 2 tablespoons butter to achieve 6 grams total fat and 210 Calories per serving.

CRAWFISH COUNTRY

Next to Hawai'i, Louisiana has to be the best "eating" place around.

The famous Louisiana chef Paul Prudhomme and I are very good friends. I enjoy visiting his hometown of Opelousas, which is about an hour and 45 minutes from Avery Island, where the McIlhenny family makes Tabasco. Out there they love to cook. In everything they go beyond the heart and one of the things they love most is that famous crawfish.

One night eight of us went to dinner at a seafood restaurant. I love telling this story. It wasn't plush—there were Formica tabletops, nothing in the way of decor—but the room was packed with people. I had to slip the host $20 to get in.

We went in and sat down. There were eight of us, looking around at the other people eating like mad. The place was like sizzling with pure joy. I opened the menu and saw fried catfish, hush puppies, and a long list of all the right things for the heart of a true food lover. "I don't know where to begin," I said. But Chef Prudhomme said, "Naw, I'm going to order."

And he did. "Give me 20 pounds of crawfish, 10 pounds of lobster, and four baskets of hush puppies."

I said, "Chef, who's going to eat all that food?"

"Sam," he said, "we have four hours. We'll work through the pile."

They had big baskets on the tables; it was the in thing. So, we jumped in and pulled off all those shells.

Now, if you want to be really proper, don't go in there because they pinch that shellfish and they suck the meat out.

It's not like going to a great fine-dining restaurant, where you would never hear a lot of sucking of shellfish going on.

I've learned a lot about the presentation of food over the years. Being a chef is like being an artist. When you create your dishes, it's important that you arrange the food on the plates and platters in a way that's colorful, and the textures and shapes harmonize.

When they see the presentation, people think, "Now here is a dish prepared by someone who knows how to cook." And it seems to make the food taste better.

It isn't that hard to do. Even if you don't have time to slice up an orange in a star shape, or peel your rind into curlicues, you can take creative shortcuts. Try opening a can of mandarin oranges and arranging the slices across a plate. It dresses up any dish, and it's fun. Or cut the tops off of raw broccoli and line them up around a serving of rice like they're a little grove of trees. Your family will love it and love you for the little time you took to make their meal a visual treat.

Try it a few times and you'll find it gets really addictive — you want to keep doing more of it, creating a pleasant scene with your food.

Of course finally it will have to taste good. That's what I learned in Louisiana, where everything came heaped in baskets. Oh, the baskets made for a fun presentation, I guess. But the focus there was on how well that great bayou food was cooked. That's the first thing people care about. So make sure it's good first, and then dress it up. That's the order of business in my restaurants. But no worry when you cook at home — both the preparation and presentation are easy.

Tsukiji Fish Market's version of crawfish.

COOL SUMMER NIGHT CIOPPINO

MAKES 12 SERVINGS

Cool summer nights call for a seafood cioppino, which is basically the kitchen sink in a pot. You dip the scoop in and heaven knows what you're going to bring up.

1 ¼ pounds firm white fish ('ahi, or yellowfin tuna; mahimahi, or dolphinfish; or ono, or wahoo)
2 ½ cups fat-free chicken stock
2 cups clam juice
¼ cup olive oil
1 tablespoon minced garlic
1 Maui onion, thinly sliced
1 cup thinly sliced celery
1 cup julienned red bell pepper
1 large fresh tomato, diced
1 pound shrimp (about 21 to 25)

¼ pound clams or mussels, shells scrubbed and rinsed
1 cup white wine
1 cup chopped fresh basil
1 Hawaiian red chile pepper, seeded and chopped (or ¼ teaspoon red chile pepper flakes)
Pinch saffron
1 spiny lobster (1 pound), cleaned and cut in half
Salt and pepper to taste

CUT FISH IN 1-INCH CUBES.

IN A LARGE POT, combine chicken stock, clam juice and wine; bring to a boil.

IN ANOTHER LARGE POT, heat oil and sauté garlic, onion, celery, bell pepper and tomato 2 or 3 minutes — adding fish, shrimp and clams. Add wine and cook 2 minutes more. Add hot stock, basil, chile pepper, saffron and lobster. Adjust seasoning with salt and pepper. Cook 8 minutes or until lobster is done.

SERVE WITH FRESH HOMEMADE BREAD.

Approximate nutrient content per serving, based on ¼ teaspoon total added salt: 180 Calories, 6 grams total fat, 1 grams saturated fat, 90 milligrams cholesterol, 450 milligrams sodium, 4 grams carbohydrate, and 24 grams protein.

BRAISED COLOSSAL SHRIMP WITH BLACK BEAN SAUCE

186

MAKES 4 SERVINGS

Black beans bring out the best in fresh seafood; they have that salty and fermented wild flavor. The flavor is catching on; some chefs are now preparing a black bean butter sauce.

1 to 2 tablespoons salted fermented black
   beans
2 pounds colossal shrimp (8 to 10 pieces
   per pound)
1/2 cup julienned green bell pepper
1/2 cup julienned onion
1 garlic clove

3 tablespoons canola oil
1/2 teaspoon salt
1 cup chicken stock
1 teaspoon soy sauce
Dash pepper
1 tablespoon cornstarch
2 tablespoons water

SOAK BLACK BEANS, rinse and drain; mash with garlic. Mix cornstarch and cold water to make a paste; set aside.

IN A WOK, heat oil on medium-high heat. Stir-fry black-bean mixture and salt a few times to heat through. Add shrimp and brown lightly. Stir in stock, heat quickly and simmer 3 or 4 minutes. Add onion and bell pepper, and simmer covered for 2 minutes or until done. Stir in soy sauce and pepper. Stir in cornstarch paste to thicken.

Approximate nutrient content per serving, based on
2 tablespoons black beans: 270 Calories, 13 grams total
fat, 1.5 grams saturated fat, 270 milligrams cholesterol,
90 milligrams sodium, 6 grams carbohydrate, and
31 grams protein.

*Lower-fat tip: Substitute fat-free chicken stock and use only
1 tablespoon canola oil to achieve 5 grams total fat and
200 Calories per serving.*

BAKED COCONUT SHRIMP 'ANAEHO'OMALU BAY

MAKES 4 SERVINGS

1 pound shrimp (about 16 to 20)
2 tablespoons olive oil
1 tablespoon soy sauce
1 tablespoon minced ginger
2 teaspoons minced fresh herbs
    (combination of basil, dill
    and/or thyme)
1 clove garlic, minced

Filling:
    ¹/₂ cup soft butter
    ¹/₄ cup bread crumbs
    ¹/₄ cup fresh coconut, grated or
        sliced very thin
    2 tablespoons freshly grated
        Parmesan cheese
    ¹/₂ teaspoon paprika
    Salt and pepper to taste

We were camping at 'Anaeho'omalu Bay north of Kona and I created this in an aluminum pan on the hibachi. It was a hit. These things don't happen by planning ...

PREHEAT OVEN to 350 degrees.

PEEL AND DEVEIN SHRIMP, leaving tails on. To butterfly shrimp, slice the underside, then spread and flatten. In a mixing bowl, combine olive oil, soy sauce, ginger, herbs and garlic; marinate butterflied shrimp in mixture 20 to 30 minutes.

COMBINE FILLING ingredients and press 1 teaspoon or more into each shrimp. Place stuffed shrimps on lightly greased baking sheet. Bake until shrimp is pink and stuffing is lightly browned, 10 to 12 minutes.

Approximate nutrient content per serving, based on
¹/₄ teaspoon total added salt: 380 Calories, 34 grams total
fat, 18 grams saturated fat, 200 milligrams cholesterol,
830 milligrams sodium, 4 grams carbohydrate, and
17 grams protein.

*Lower-fat tip: Use only 2 teaspoons olive oil and ¹/₄ cup butter
to achieve 18 grams total fat and 240 Calories per serving.*

STIR-FRIED LOBSTER AND TOMATOES WITH BLACK BEANS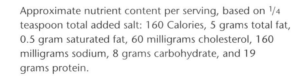

MAKES 6 SERVINGS

2 teaspoons salted fermented black beans
3 lobster tails (4 to 6 ounces each)
1 clove garlic, minced
1/2 teaspoon minced fresh ginger
1/4 cup chicken stock
1 tablespoon sherry
1 teaspoon soy sauce
1 teaspoon brown sugar

1/4 teaspoon salt
Dash pepper
2 teaspoons cornstarch
3 tablespoons water
2 tablespoons canola oil
2 fresh tomatoes, peeled and diced

This recipe sets the tone. Then, people can prepare it with crab or clams or oysters or shrimp or scallops or even chicken. It all works, I'm told.

SOAK BLACK BEANS in water. Meanwhile, cut each lobster tail into 8 cubes, to produce 24 lobster pieces. Drain black beans and mash with garlic and ginger.

IN ONE CUP, blend chicken stock, sherry, soy sauce, brown sugar, salt and pepper. In another cup, mix cornstarch and cold water to make a paste.

IN A WOK, heat oil over medium-high heat and stir-fry black-bean mixture 30 seconds. Add lobster and stir-fry 2 to 4 minutes. Add sherry-soy mixture and cook 1 minute, then stir in cornstarch paste to thicken. Fold in tomatoes and heat through. Serve over hot steamed rice.

Approximate nutrient content per serving, based on 1/4 teaspoon total added salt: 160 Calories, 5 grams total fat, 0.5 gram saturated fat, 60 milligrams cholesterol, 160 milligrams sodium, 8 grams carbohydrate, and 19 grams protein.

190

SMOKED SHRIMP WITH MANGO SALSA

MAKES 4 SERVINGS

Try a different and challenging preparation that gives juicy shrimp the mouth-watering accents of smoking and pineapple. Add a snappy mango salsa.

1 ½ pounds large shrimp
   (about 31 to 37 pieces)
Salt and pepper to taste
1 tablespoon minced garlic
1 teaspoon brown sugar

Kiawe (algaroba) chips or other
   preferred wood chips
2 pieces pineapple rind (outer peel)
Aluminum foil

Mango Salsa, see below

SEASON SHRIMP WITH SALT, pepper, garlic and brown sugar. In a heavy baking pan, spread kiawe chips and pineapple rind. Put a rack in pan. Place pan directly on stove burner over high heat. When chips start to smoke, place shrimp on rack and seal pan tightly with foil. Reduce heat to low and cook shrimps until done, 10 to 15 minutes. Serve with Mango Salsa.

Approximate nutrient content per serving with ¼ cup salsa, based on ¼ teaspoon total added salt in salsa: 140 Calories, 1.5 grams total fat, 0.5 gram saturated fat, 200 milligrams cholesterol, 400 milligrams sodium, 9 grams carbohydrate, and 22 grams protein.

MANGO SALSA

MAKES 3 CUPS

2 cups chopped fresh mango
½ cup chopped red onion
½ cup chopped fresh basil
¼ cup chopped red bell pepper
2 tablespoons chopped cilantro

2 tablespoon sugar
1 Hawaiian red chile pepper,
   seeded and minced
½ teaspoon powdered cumin
Salt and pepper to taste

COMBINE ALL INGREDIENTS;
blend well.

Approximate nutrient content per ¼-cup serving: 30 Calories, no fat, no cholesterol, 45 milligrams sodium, 8 grams carbohydrate, and no protein.

TOMATO CRAB

MAKES 6 SERVINGS

1 whole crab
2 tablespoons canola oil
4 ripe, fresh tomatoes, cut into wedges
1 cup assorted sliced vegetables,
    such as onions, celery, bell peppers
    and mushrooms

1 tablespoon chopped garlic
2 tablespoons soy sauce
2 tablespoons oyster sauce
1 cup chicken stock
1 teaspoon tomato paste

You've heard of beef tomato. Well, this is "crab tomato." It's simple, good, easy and different.

TO PREPARE CRAB, snap off top shell, and clean out gills and mouthparts. Cut body in 4 to 6 pieces.

IN A HEAVY SKILLET, heat oil and cook crab 1 minute. Add remaining ingredients and cook 8 to 10 minutes.

Approximate nutrient content per serving, based on 4 ounces crabmeat total: 100 Calories, 6 grams total fat, 0.5 gram saturated fat, 20 milligrams cholesterol, 800 milligrams sodium, 6 grams carbohydrate, and 7 grams protein.

Lower-fat tip: Substitute fat-free chicken stock and use only 1 tablespoon canola oil to achieve 3 grams total fat and 80 Calories per serving.

Live Dungeness crabs.

'Āina Kepanī
(Sam in Japan)

194

One of the wonderful perks about having a restaurant in Japan is being able to visit. Tokyo is a remarkable place. There are so many aspects of Japanese cuisine that have become part of Hawai'i's food traditions — soy sauce, tofu, seafood, colorful vegetables, fresh foods cooked briefly, and oh yes, the rice.

You can't beat the rice in Japan. It's the best rice in the world, hands down. They have short grain rice that looks fat. When you eat it, it has a little crunch. It's snappy. It's very good and very white — like eating pearls.

Restaurants have glass containers of soy sauce on their tables. Shoyu's become a staple condiment in Hawai'i, and sits on our kitchen tables, too. Everybody has their favorite brand. It doesn't matter what anybody says, the brand of shoyu does make a difference. The sodium levels aren't the same, so the tastes vary. I use different brands for different effects in my cooking.

That worker is catching a big one at Tsukiji Fish Market!

I give the Japanese credit. They take pride in what they do, and their work ethic is amazing. Everywhere I visit in Japan I'm knocked out by the cleanliness. Even the alleys in downtown Tokyo are so free of rubbish that food vendors sell their delicacies from little carts right in the alley, and people in business suits walk there like it's a main thoroughfare.

TERIYAKI SQUID TOKYO STYLE

MAKES 4 (PUPU) SERVINGS

**1 pound whole fresh squid
(can substitute cuttlefish)**

Marinade:
¹/₃ cup soy sauce
¹/₄ cup sugar

1 tablespoon sake
1 tablespoon olive oil
1 tablespoon grated ginger
1 clove garlic, grated

*Every now and then
we hook big squid out
here in Kona at night-
time. Just marinate them
in a little teriyaki and
throw them on the
hibachi. Ho, real good.*

TO CLEAN SQUID, separate tail-and-fin sections from tentacles. Remove ink sac, innards, roundish cartilage and cuttlebone. Rinse and drain.

COMBINE MARINADE ingredients and marinate squid 1 or 2 hours in refrigerator. Grill or broil for a few minutes on each side.

Approximate nutrient content per serving: 200 Calories, 5 grams total fat, 1 gram saturated fat, 265 milligrams cholesterol, at least 1,200 milligrams sodium, 17 grams carbohydrate, and 20 grams protein.

🍃 Low-fat tip: Use only 1 teaspoon olive oil to achieve 3 grams total fat and 180 Calories per serving.

ONO CARPACCIO WITH HOT GINGER PEPPER OIL

196

MAKES 4 SERVINGS

This recipe developed when I used ginger pesto on sashimi. The combination has a sweet, fresh medley of flavors. Then I said it needed a kick, so I poured spicy oil on top. Ho! Winner.

1-pound block very fresh ono
   (wahoo) fillet
1 ½ cups finely shredded raw vegetables
   (cabbage, carrot, jicama, daikon, or
   Asian turnip; or beet curls)

Hot Ginger-Pepper Oil:
   ½ cup canola oil
   ¼ cup minced ginger
   ¼ cup minced shallots
   ¼ cup lightly packed cilantro, minced
   ½ teaspoon red chile pepper flakes
   ¼ teaspoon salt
   ⅛ teaspoon white pepper

CUT RAW FISH in thin slices of desired size, such as 2 ½ by 1 ¾ by ¼ inch.

TO PREPARE Hot Ginger-Pepper Oil, heat oil in a small saucepan. Add salt and cook 2 or 3 minutes. Stir in ginger, shallots, cilantro, chile pepper flakes, salt and white pepper. Makes ¾ cup.

ON A SMALL PLATTER or an individual plate, make a bed of vegetables. Arrange raw ono slices on top. Spoon Hot Ginger-Pepper Oil over fish.

Approximate nutrient content per serving fish only:
220 Calories, 9 grams total fat, 2.5 grams saturated fat,
55 milligrams cholesterol, 120 milligrams sodium,
9 grams carbohydrate, and 25 grams protein.

Approximate nutrient content per 1-tablespoon
serving pepper oil: 80 Calories, 9 grams total fat,
0.5 gram saturated fat, no cholesterol, 90 milligrams
sodium, 1 gram carbohydrate, and no protein.

Lower-fat tip: Use spiced oil sparingly.

SIMMER SHOYU SUGAR BUTTERFISH WITH VEGETABLES

MAKES 4 SERVINGS

Butterfish is an oily fish. When you simmer or poach it in a sugar-shoyu mixture and add vegetables, it's like nishime (Japanese stew). Onolicious!

Nonstick vegetable-oil cooking spray
1 pound butterfish (black cod)
⅓ cup soy sauce
2 ½ tablespoons sugar
1 tablespoon water
½ cup julienned carrot

½ cup julienned celery
½ bunch fresh watercress,
  cut in 1 ½-inch lengths
4 stalks green onion, cut in 1-inch lengths
1 block (20 ounces) firm tofu,
  drained and cubed

SPRAY FISH with up to 5 seconds of nonstick vegetable-oil cooking spray. In a large skillet over medium heat, sauté butterfish about 1 minute on each side; remove to a plate.

MIX SUGAR, soy sauce and 1 tablespoon water. Add one-half of this mixture to skillet along with carrots and celery; cook 6 to 8 minutes. Push carrots and celery to one side and return butterfish to skillet. Pour remaining soy-sauce mixture over fish and vegetables; cook 5 minutes. Add watercress stems and cook 1 minute. Add onions, tofu and watercress leaves; cook 2 minutes. Do not overcook.

Approximate nutrient content per serving: 440 Calories, 23 grams total fat, 6 grams saturated fat, 75 milligrams cholesterol, at least 1,300 milligrams sodium, 18 grams carbohydrate, and 46 grams protein.

Lower-fat tip: Substitute "lite" tofu to achieve 14 grams total fat and 320 Calories per serving.

SAM IN JAPAN

One of the most exciting lu'au I ever gave was the May 1996 opening of my Tokyo restaurant. I have a few friends in Japan—David Stant, classmate Robert and Mona Kahawai'i, and my wife's classmate Larry Weeber, whom I wanted to see. There was also the Hawai'i contingent that came with me for the opening. An inaugural lu'au would be a way to begin with good mana.

I also invited the Hawai'i-born sumotori (sumo wrestlers). We'd met before only briefly, but if they were like all the other local boys away from home, I knew they'd appreciate the chance for some local food.

I thought I'd be comfortable with them, since we all share the same kind of build (although when I got right next to them I felt really small—they totally dwarfed me).

I wasn't sure what they expected or how much at home they'd feel. Some of them were major celebrities, and they would be around people they hardly knew.

Let me tell you, my apprehensions vanished when the big boys stepped out of their vans. I was hugged and greeted like a long-time-no-see high school buddy. Within minutes the gathering became a local folks' get-together away from home.

It was a great experience sitting and breaking bread with them as colleagues, like nobody's better than the other—yet knowing in my mind that yokozuna (grand champion) Akebono (27-year-old Chad Rowan of Waimanalo) is as big in the sumo world as Michael Jordan is in America. In Japan people scream when they touch him, or any of the Hawai'i sumo entourage—Musashimaru (Fiamalu Penitani), Konishiki (Salevaa Atisanoe), Yamato (George Kalima), Nanfu (Kaleo Kekauoha), and the other up-and-comers. I was really, really proud to be with them that evening.

They invited me to watch their training the next day and to eat at their sumo stable. I sat with them and ate "chanko nabe," which was delicious. It was in a big sukiyaki-type pot—18 inches across, 9 inches deep—over a burner. To the bubbling broth they added boneless chicken, tofu, aburaage (fried bean curd), Chinese cabbage, and

Musashimaru made me feel kind of small.
bean sprouts. The high-ranking

sumotori were the first to partake of the chanko-nabe delicacies over three to five bowls of rice. Then, the lower-ranked sumotori had their turn. Finally, the lowest-ranked sumotori took their place by the pot.

I asked why they ate in sequence. They said it's part of the Buddhist religious ritual surrounding their sport since ancient times. Every wrestler must wait his turn.

The highlight of my visit was the twinkle in their eyes when we talked about home. Massive Salevaa straddled a chair, his huge arm over the chair back, and he listened and swayed to Island music. He said, "Hah, that's what I miss—Hawaiian sounds." Behind the spotlights and popularity, these are just local guys in their twenties. But I admired their positive disposition about who they are and their receptivity to the Japanese public and media.

Watching them at the sumo stables made me appreciate sumo in the sports world. It's a tough sport requiring sprint-speed and agility, as well as size. These men have to be in excellent physical condition.

They told me they need to tap their feelings within, to use gut strength in competition. They wanted to put forth their all, to extract beyond 100 percent. It is all there inside of them, especially their Hawaiianness.

BAKED TERIYAKI BUTTERFISH WITH TOFU

200

MAKES 6 SERVINGS

You know, butterfish sells itself. What's really remarkable is when you combine tofu with it and the marinade. Let me tell you: It's like never-ending butterfish!

1 pound butterfish (black cod)
   steaks or fillets
Salt and pepper to taste
Pinch red chile pepper flakes
Flour
2 tablespoons olive oil
1 block (20 ounces) firm tofu, cubed
Chopped green onions

Sauce:
¼ cup soy sauce
3 tablespoons sugar
1-inch piece fresh ginger, grated
1 clove garlic, minced

SEASON BOTH SIDES of fish with salt, pepper and red chile pepper flakes, then dust with flour. In a frying pan, heat olive oil and sauté fillets about 3 minutes on each side.

IN A BAKING DISH, place tofu cubes and arrange fish on top. Combine sauce ingredients and pour over all. Bake 20 minutes at 300 degrees. Garnish with green onions.

Approximate nutrient content per serving, based on no added salt: 330 Calories, 19 grams total fat, 4.5 grams saturated fat, 50 milligrams cholesterol, 690 milligrams sodium, 14 grams carbohydrate, and 30 grams protein.

Lower-fat tip: Substitute a "lite" tofu and use only 2 teaspoons canola oil to achieve 10 grams total fat and 230 Calories per serving.

THE ALL-IN-ONE POT DINNER—THE "NABE"

MAKES 18 SERVINGS

1 pound salmon bellies
1 tablespoon sake
1 block (20 ounces) tofu
1 daikon (Asian radish)
2 taro corms
8 leaves won bok (Napa cabbage)
8 stalks watercress
3 stalks green onion
⅓ pound fresh enoki mushrooms
    (enokitake)
12 fresh shiitake mushrooms, halved
Bean sprouts, any quantity
½ fish cake, sliced
1 package (2 ounces) long rice,
    soaked overnight in water
2 packages (7 ounces each) fresh udon
    (thick noodles)

Soup:
1 whole piece dashi konbu (packaged
    dried kelp), cut in 4-inch pieces,
    available in Asian section of markets
8 cups light clam stock
½ cup dashi-no-moto (Japanese powdered
    sea-soup base)
½ cup miso (fermented soybean paste)
2 tablespoons mirin (glutinous-rice wine)
2 tablespoons sake (Japanese rice wine)
2 tablespoons soy sauce
1-inch piece fresh ginger, crushed

I liked this dish when I went to Japan; so I want to share it. I was impressed watching the sumotori keep adding ingredients — like a never-ending shabu shabu.

CUT SALMON BELLIES in bite-size pieces and sprinkle with sake. Cut tofu in 1 ¼-inch cubes. Peel daikon and taro, and cut in bite-size pieces. Cut green onion, watercress and won bok in 2-inch lengths. Trim and discard hard root ends of enoki mushrooms.

TO PREPARE SOUP: Soak konbu in water 30 minutes; drain. In a large stockpot, cook clam stock and konbu on low heat. Just before stock reaches boiling point, remove and discard konbu. Bring stock to a boil and add dashi-no-moto. Reduce heat and simmer, adding miso, mirin, sake, soy sauce and ginger.

IN A JAPANESE DONABE POT over a flame, arrange salmon, tofu, daikon, taro, shiitake, fish cake and long rice. Add soup and cook. When vegetables are done, add watercress, green onion and enoki mushrooms.

AS A FINALE after eating the fish, tofu and vegetables, boil udon in remaining rich soup broth and serve.

Approximate nutrient content per serving, based on ¼ teaspoon total added salt: 140 Calories, 4 grams total fat, 0.5 gram saturated fat, 20 milligrams cholesterol, 690 milligrams sodium, 15 grams carbohydrate, and 11 grams protein.

202

Scenes from Sam Choy's Tokyo restaurant opening night and Tsukiji Fish Market.

1. *Musashimaru (Fiamalu Penitani of Wai'anae) samples the delectables.*

2. *Yamato (George Kalima of Waimanalo), left, Akebono (Chad Rowan of Waimanalo) and chef Dutch O'Neil enjoy a light moment.*

3. *Akebono and I are set to enjoy a feast.*

4. *Sam Jr. and I check out a fresh specimen at Tsukiji Fish Market.*

5. *Mr. Aisuke Goto and Hitoshi Goto greet Musashimaru.*

6. *Nanfu (Kaleo Kekauoha), right, anchors a table at opening night festivities.*

7. *A Tsukiji fish seller and I give shaka signs.*

8. *Konishiki (Salevaa Atisanoe) wears a colorful signature kimono.*

9. *I enjoyed seeing all those Tsukiji bins filled with seafoods.*

10. *From left, Daiski (Percy Kipapa), Sam Jr., David and Lorie Stant with keikis, Koryu (Eric Cosier, rear), myself, Musashimaru and Nanfu in front of the new restaurant.*

NA MEAʻAI MOMONA
(DESSERTS)

Hawai'i has a lot of unbelievable dessert flavors — the tropical fruit tastes of mango, papaya, guava, pineapple, and banana; the crunch of macadamia nuts and toasted coconut; and the aromatic richness of island-grown coffee.

Some favorite island desserts are macadamia nut cream pie, chocolate dobash, and that famous *haupia*, or coconut pudding. There are even ones we talk about but never get around to making, like *kulolo* (taro-coconut milk dessert). I was fortunate to be raised near the Stant family, which made *kulolo* every Wednesday. It was their family business and the *kulolo* was excellent.

Haupia — the traditional Hawaiian coconut pudding — is topped with a new twist, mango marmalade.

I remember four *pa kini* — big washtubs — filled with taro. Elena Stant, my friend Kawika's mom, would sit for hours grating and grating, first the taro and then the coconut. I helped her get the coconut milk for "Elena's *kulolo*." She loaded a cheesecloth with grated coconut meat and told me to twist. As I squeezed and twisted, the thick, creamy coconut milk dripped into the one-gallon glass jar she put under my hands. In exchange for my help, she gave me two *kulolo* bundles to take home. I've never tasted *kulolo* as good as the Stant family's and I wish they would make it again.

My favorite dessert is my wife Carol's double-crusted banana pie. It's unreal good. The best.

HILO HAUPIA SQUARES

MAKES 24 SERVINGS

Macadamia cookie crust:
- 1 cup butter
- 2 cups flour
- ¼ cup light brown sugar
- ½ cup finely chopped
    macadamia nuts

Haupia mixture:
- 2 cans (12 ounces each)
    frozen coconut milk, thawed
- 2 cups milk
- 1 cup sugar
- ½ cup cornstarch
- 1 cup toasted sweetened flaked coconut
- 8 ounces chopped fresh Waimea
    strawberries (optional)

Bake a cookie crust and pour haupia on top of that. It's really, really 'ono (delicious). The macadamia nut cookie crust adds a nice flavor touch.

PREHEAT OVEN to 350 degrees.

IN A MEDIUM mixing bowl, cut butter into flour with a pastry blender. Stir in brown sugar and macadamia nuts, and mix well. Press dough into a 13-by-9-inch baking pan. Bake 15 minutes or until lightly browned.

IN A LARGE SAUCEPAN, mix coconut milk with milk. Mix sugar with cornstarch, and stir into unheated coconut-milk mixture. Cook on medium heat, stirring frequently, until mixture thickens. Pour mixture over baked crust. Chill. Garnish with coconut and, if desired, strawberries.

COOKING TIP:
Oven-toast flaked coconut on a dry baking sheet in a preheated 325-degree oven, turning coconut occasionally, until lightly browned.

Approximate nutrient content per serving with strawberries: 260 Calories, 18 grams total fat, 12 grams saturated fat, 25 milligrams cholesterol, 105 milligrams sodium, 25 grams carbohydrate, and 3 grams protein.

Lower-fat tips: Substitute low-fat coconut milk (1 gram fat per tablespoon) and convert cookie-crust ingredients (except use only ½ cup butter) into a crumb topping to achieve 9 grams total fat and 170 Calories per serving.

MACADAMIA NUT DRIED-PAPAYA "ALWAYS TASTES GREAT" BREAD PUDDING

MAKES 16 SERVINGS

2 cups Portuguese, "Hawaiian" or Easter
    sweet-bread cubes, day old or older
1 1/2 cups heavy cream
1 cup diced dried papaya, preferably
    with no added sugar
Flour

3/4 cup sugar
3 eggs, beaten
1/2 cup chopped macadamia nuts
1/4 cup melted butter
1 teaspoon vanilla
1/2 teaspoon salt
Dash cinnamon

You get creamy custard from the eggs, chewy sweetness from the dried papaya, and crunchiness from the macadamia nuts on top. It doesn't get any better.

SOAK BREAD IN CREAM. Dust papaya with flour so fruits won't sink in pudding. Combine remaining ingredients and bread mixture. Pour mixture in buttered 9-by-9-by-2-inch baking dish. Bake 45 minutes at 375 degrees.

BONUS DESSERT TIP:

If you like vanilla sauce—crème anglaise—here's a way to make it that's so easy. A Waldorf-Astoria chef taught me this trick one evening when they were caught without their dessert sauce. What he did, and what you can do, is to melt leftover vanilla ice cream in a saucepan or pot. Soften it up and add milk or half-and-half. Bring it to a low boil without letting it boil over, and add a touch of cornstarch and water—for a nice glaze. Vanilla ice cream has an unusually large amount of vanilla to carry the flavor, so this makes a strong, excellent sauce. It can fool even the most taste-sensitive gourmet. Try it.

Approximate nutrient content per serving bread pudding: 210 Calories, 16 grams total fat, 8 grams saturated fat, 85 milligrams cholesterol, 210 milligrams sodium, 16 grams carbohydrate, and 3 grams protein.

Lower-fat tip: Substitute half-and-half in place of the cream; spray baking pan with nonstick vegetable-oil cooking spray; and use only 1/4 cup macadamia nuts to achieve 9 grams total fat and 150 calories per serving.

CHOCOLATE MACADAMIA CREAM CHEESE PIE

MAKES 10 SERVINGS

This is my sister Wai Sun Choy's favorite. Dessert is her category. This is different, it's good. It's the Kona version of "Death by Chocolate".

8 ounces cream cheese
4 ounces sugar (1/2 cup plus 1 tablespoon)
1 teaspoon vanilla extract
2 tablespoons liquid egg substitute (Egg Eze)
6 ounces semi-sweet chocolate morsels, melted

6 ounces unsalted macadamia nuts (1 1/2 cups), chopped or diced
2 egg whites
4 ounces sugar (1/2 cup plus 1 tablespoon)
2 cups whipped cream
Chocolate shavings
9-inch baked Oreo-cookie crust (optional)

WITH AN ELECTRIC MIXER, cream the cream cheese, sugar and vanilla. Beat in egg substitute until smooth. Blend melted chocolate and macadamia nuts into cream-cheese mixture.

USE MIXER TO WHIP egg whites with sugar to form stiff peaks; fold into chocolate mixture thoroughly. Then, fold 1 cup of whipped cream into mixture.

IF DESIRED, pour pie filling into Oreo cookie crust and refrigerate at least 8 hours. Top with whipped cream and chocolate shavings. Or, pour mixture into individual serving cups, and top with whipped cream and chocolate shavings. Keep this dessert refrigerated at all times.

Approximate nutrient content per serving: 490 Calories, 37 grams total fat, 16 grams saturated fat, 100 milligrams cholesterol, 90 milligrams sodium, 39 grams carbohydrate, and 4 grams protein.

Lower-fat tip: Substitute "light" cream cheese and Cool Whip low-fat frozen dessert topping (in place of whipped cream), and use only 3/4 cup chopped macadamia nuts to achieve 21 grams total fat and 360 Calories per serving.

Macadamia nuts on the tree.

Mango Bread

Makes 2 Loaves, or 24 Slices

2 cups flour
2 teaspoons baking soda
1 teaspoon baking powder
2 teaspoons cinnamon
3 eggs, well beaten
3/4 cup canola oil
1 1/2 cups sugar

2 cups peeled and diced fresh mango
   (see note)
1/2 cup raisins
1/2 cup chopped macadamia nuts or
   walnuts
1/2 cup grated coconut

I like mango bread. Here in the Islands, it's a tradition to make it and give it away. You can make French toast with it. You can toast it... it's fun sitting around peeling mangoes.

PREHEAT OVEN to 350 degrees. Grease and flour two 9-by-5-inch loaf pans. Sift flour, baking soda, baking powder and cinnamon.

IN A LARGE MIXING BOWL, combine eggs, oil, sugar, mango, raisins, nuts and coconut; combine with dry ingredients and blend well. Pour into loaf pans and bake until breads test done, 45 to 60 minutes.

NOTE: *Can substitute mashed banana, grated carrot or diced papaya in place of mango.*

Approximate nutrient content per slice: 200 Calories, 11 grams total fat, 2 grams saturated fat, 25 milligrams cholesterol, 135 milligrams sodium, 26 grams carbohydrate, and 6 grams protein.

Lower-fat tip: Substitute applesauce for oil to achieve 4 grams total fat and 150 Calories per serving.

A bumper crop of mangoes.

MANGO GUAVA SORBET

212

MAKES 10 (1/2-CUP) SERVINGS

Here's a good way to use an overabundance of mangoes. We always have plenty of common mangoes in Kona. People bring them by the boxes. Some sell, some give.

2 large overripe mangoes, peeled
    and cut in 1-inch cubes
1 can (6 ounces) frozen guava-nectar
    concentrate, thawed
Sugar to taste

IN A FOOD PROCESSOR or blender, machine process all ingredients to form a purée. Freeze 45 minutes or until icy.

REMOVE MIXTURE from freezer and whip with a wire whisk. Refreeze 45 minutes.

REMOVE MIXTURE from freezer and machine process 30 seconds. Refreeze until time to serve. Tastes great on a hot summer day.

Approximate nutrient content per serving: 80 Calories,
no fat, no cholesterol, no sodium, 24 grams carbohydrate,
and 1 gram protein.

THREE-FRUIT SHERBET 🍃

MAKES 8 (1/2-CUP) SERVINGS

I freeze the fruit purée until it's like slush. Then whip it with a whisk and refreeze. I like to go through this process three times; it comes out really smooth.

1 ripe medium mango, peeled and
    seed removed
1 1/2 cans (6 ounces each) passion-fruit
    nectar concentrate

1 can (13 ounces) pineapple chunks
    with syrup
1 cup instant nonfat milk powder
1 tablespoon sugar

IN A FOOD PROCESSOR or blender, combine all ingredients and blend well. Pour into a pan and freeze. Great for the hottest times of the summer.

Approximate nutrient content per serving: 130 Calories, no fat, no cholesterol, 45 milligrams sodium, 31 grams carbohydrate, and 3 grams protein.

HIBACHI PINEAPPLE SPEARS

MAKES 4 SERVINGS

Light and refreshing! (Another Patrick Choy creation)

2-pound fresh pineapple, cut in thin spears
    (can substitute fresh mango or
    guava slices)

Aluminum foil
4 tablespoons brown sugar
4 tablespoons butter
Freshly ground pepper (optional)

LAY 3 OR 4 PINEAPPLE spears on a piece of foil per person. Top fruit with a sprinkling of light brown sugar and a small butter dollop. Seal foil packet. Grill on both sides until sugar melts. Open foil and, if desired, top fruits with a little freshly ground pepper.

Approximate nutrient content per serving: 210 Calories, 12 grams total fat, 7 grams saturated fat, 30 milligrams cholesterol, 125 milligrams sodium, 28 grams carbohydrate, and 1 gram protein.

🍃 *Low-fat tip: Substitute butter-flavored nonstick vegetable-oil cooking spray in place of butter to achieve 3 grams total fat and 125 Calories per serving.*

MOM'S STORY: 'HE NEVER LOOKED BACK'

It's a hard job being a parent. My husband and I tried to give the kids opportunities. We've been fortunate that all our children have done real well in life. They're all happy, and that's what's important. Sam was always a good boy. But you know, Dad and I didn't think he would become a chef.

He was around food all the time when he was little. My husband had a catering business and a restaurant, so we had to have the kids' help. It was tough in those days. It didn't seem like Sam enjoyed cooking much. Whenever we asked him to clean the vegetables or cut the meat, he made that "tssst" sound — the one kids do when they don't like what you are saying. I didn't really know what he wanted to be when he got older. Cooking didn't seem to be on his mind much.

When he graduated from high school, he really wanted to go away to college, play football and see the world. So we sent him to Columbia Basin Junior College in Washington state. He was gone only about a month when we get this phone call. "Ma," he says, "I gotta come home."

"What's wrong, boy?" I asked. "You too cold?"

"I'm homesick," he said.

"I think you're lovesick!"

"I just want to come home."

So, at the end of the quarter, here he comes, back to La'ie.

His dad was so mad. "We send you away and you come back so fast," he scolded. "What you gonna do now, go with the boys up the North Shore and surf and fish and motocross all day?"

My husband didn't fool around when it came to work. One night he told me, "You tell Sam to find a job, go in the service, or go back to school."

The next day I was looking through the Advertiser. There was an article about Kapi'olani Community College and how they started a new program in food service for young people. "Sam," I said, "let's go down and look at this school. They have some new food classes."

He hated driving to Honolulu. "No, never mind," he told me. "I'm going to find a job here."

"I'll drive you," I told him.

He knows me. I never offer to drive anybody anywhere. So we went.

We got to the Pensacola campus and there was a long line. Sam doesn't like to wait. He fidgeted and fidgeted. He was making me nervous. "Go sit over there," I said. There were some kids under a tree. He walked over and began talking story like they were old friends. (Just like he does today.) I had to stand in line and register him.

When I got to the front of the line, I motioned him to come get his packet and stuff. He was all nuha. "I hope I like this. I'm doing it for your sake," he told me.

I said, "I hope so, too, because Pa is not going to support you if you stay at home just fuss around." Then I went over to another line to get him a parking permit.

The following week classes started. One week later he said, "Ma, I think I found something I like."

I said, "You did?"

He said, "Yup."

I said, "Oh, thank God."

He went right through the program. I never saw a guy so happy as he was with school. He never looked back from that day 'til today.

You know, sometimes, kids need a push. To think, Sam's a famous chef all because I read something in the newspaper.

I'm proud of my Sam.

Patrick Choy with Clairemoana Meyer Choy.

HIBACHI BANANAS FOSTER

MAKES 6 SERVINGS

Caution: Only experienced flambé cooks should try the flambé step. And make sure the ocean is close, in case the flambé is too big!
(A Patrick Choy dessert)

1 stick unsalted butter ($^1/_2$ cup)
1 cup dark brown sugar
$^1/_4$ cup banana liqueur
6 ripe bananas, sliced and doused with
   lemon juice to prevent discoloration
Disposable aluminum pan
Aluminum foil
3 or 4 splashes 151-proof rum

Optional:
   Vanilla ice cream
   Whipped cream
   Toasted macadamia nuts

KITCHEN "PREP": In a sauté pan on low heat, melt butter until it bubbles lightly. Stir in brown sugar and cook until mixture bubbles again. Stir in banana liqueur and banana slices, and transfer mixture to a disposable aluminum pan. Wrap tightly with foil and pack for a picnic.

PICNIC-TABLESIDE COOKING: Place foil-wrapped pan on hot hibachi and grill until you can smell sugar cooking and caramelizing on bananas; do not burn sugar. Remove foil to monitor cooking. When sugar mixture glazes nicely over bananas, splash with rum. Use tongs to tilt pan slightly toward embers so sauce will ignite.

IF DESIRED, spoon flambéed bananas over vanilla ice cream and top with whipped cream and toasted macadamia nuts.

THIS DESSERT can be prepared at home in a sauté pan on a gas stove; if on an electric stove, use a lighter or match to flambé rum.

Approximate nutrient content per serving fruit only:
480 Calories, 16 grams total fat, 10 grams saturated fat,
40 milligrams cholesterol, 170 milligrams sodium,
71 grams carbohydrate, and 1 gram protein.

Lower-fat tip: Indulge in only half of this dessert.

GRILLED TROPICAL FRUITS 🍃

MAKES 20 (¹/₂-CUP) SERVINGS

1 whole fresh pineapple, peeled,
    cored and diced
4 ripe bananas, peeled, sliced and dipped in
    lemon juice to prevent discoloration
2 ripe mangoes, peeled and sliced
Fresh lychees (or 1 can lychees),
    pitted and halved
Disposable aluminum pan

¹/₄ cup butter (¹/₂ stick)
¹/₂ cup brown sugar
¹/₂ ounce grated fresh ginger
Aluminum foil

Optional:
    Vanilla ice cream or butter pound cake
    Toasted grated fresh coconut

Pre-pack an array of enticing fruits for a picnic, then caramelize the fruits over a hibachi. Another of brother Patrick's wonders.

KITCHEN "PREP": Combine fruits in a disposable aluminum pan and drain off all juices. In a saute pan on low heat, melt butter until it bubbles lightly. Stir in brown sugar and cook until mixture bubbles again. Drain juices from fruits again, then pour sugar mixture over fruits and sprinkle with ginger. Wrap tightly with foil and pack for a picnic.

OUTDOOR COOKING: Place foil-wrapped pan on hot hibachi and grill until you can smell sugar cooking and caramelizing on fruits; do not burn sugar. Remove foil to monitor cooking. Stir so sugar mixture glazes nicely over fruits.

IF DESIRED, spoon fruits over vanilla ice cream or butter pound cake, and top with coconut.

Approximate nutrient content per serving fruit only: 110 Calories, 2.5 grams total fat, 1.5 grams saturated fat, 5 milligrams cholesterol, 25 milligrams sodium, 24 grams carbohydrate, and 1 gram protein.

Lower-fat tip: Serve on nonfat frozen yogurt or nonfat ice cream, but remember that Calories will increase.

WINE LIST

I always urge everyone, in trying my recipes, to let their palates be their guides and to pay attention to their "inner circle of flavors" and personal tastes. My many years of experience watching people dine and listening to their comments has taught me that each person differently enjoys flavors, tastes, aromas, and textures, depending on their mood and appetite craving. The same holds true for what wine to use.

Recipe	Recommended Choice
NA PUPU A ME NA KUPA (APPETIZERS & SOUPS)	
Deep-Fried Mahimahi Macadamia Nut Fingers	Turning Leaf Chardonnay
Summer 'Ahi Tartare	Zabaco Pinot Noir
Wok Barbecue Shrimp with Pepper-Papaya-Pineapple Chutney	Gossamer Bay Zinfandel/ Turning Leaf Merlot/ Gossamer Bay Chardonnay
Wings of Wings Miso Shoyu Chicken	Gossamer Bay White Zinfandel
Crab and Shrimp Stuffed Shiitake Mushrooms with Mango Béarnaise Sauce	Turning Leaf Cabernet
Tailgate Mochi Mochi Chicken	Zabaco Chardonnay
Da Wife's Bean Soup	Turning Leaf Cabernet
Kona Seafood Chowder	Zabaco Zinfandel
Quick and "Tastes Good" Barley Soup	Gossamer Bay Zinfandel
Definitely Easy Deboned Shoyu Chicken Drumettes	Gallo Sonoma Stefani Ranch Chardonnay
Best Crabmeat Soup with Taro	Gossamer Bay Chardonnay
KA POKE (SLICE)	
Poke Patties	Turning Leaf Chardonnay
Straight Hawaiian-Style 'Inamona Poke	Turning Leaf Chardonnay
Aku Poke	Gossamer Bay Chardonnay
'Ahi Poke Salad	Turning Leaf Chardonnay
Helena Pali Opihi Limu Poke	Zabaco Chardonnay
Tako Poke	Gossamer Bay Chardonnay
Blue Pincers Poke	Zabaco Sauvignon Blanc
NA LAU 'AI (GINGER)	
Why Not? Breadfruit, Sweet Potato and Taro Salad with Crabmeat	Zabaco Sauvignon Blanc
"Wow the Neighbors" Seafood Salad	Turning Leaf White Zinfandel
Hilo Tropical Fruit Slaw	Turning Leaf Sonoma Reserve Zinfandel
Lamb Salad	Gossamer Bay Sauvignon Blanc
"The Old Sand Island Days" Ogo Pickle—"Not"	Zabaco Chardonnay

Recipe	Recommended Choice
Bella Mushroom Salad	Gallo Sonoma Laguna Ranch Chardonnay
Puna Papaya and Maui Onion Dressing	Gossamer Bay Sauvignon Blanc
KE 'AWAPUHI 'AI (GINGER)	
Ginger Clams with Black Bean Sauce	Gallo Sonoma Laguna Ranch Chardonnay
Local-Style Ginger Braised Chicken	Turning Leaf Chardonnay
Ginger Shoyu Pork	Zabaco Zinfandel/ Turning Leaf Merlot
Spicy Braised Chicken with Ginger	Turning Leaf Sonoma Reserve Zinfandel
Miso Miso Boneless Chicken Thighs with Ginger	Turning Leaf Sonoma Reserve Chardonnay
Braised Ginger Honey Chicken	Turning Leaf Pinot Noir/ Zabaco Chardonnay
Cold Chicken Tossed with Fresh Ginger Pesto	Gossamer Bay Sauvignon Blanc
Gingered Lobster	Gallo Sonoma Stefani Ranch Chardonnay
KA IPUHAO PAKE (WOK)	
Wok-Fried Lobster with Thick Soy	Anapamu Chardonnay
Wok the Chicken with Eggplant and Hot Peppers	Turning Leaf Sonoma Reserve Pinot Noir
Wok Spicy Tofu	Gossamer Bay Sauvignon Blanc
Wok Pork, Pineapple Barbecue Sauce and Lychees	Anapamu Chardonnay
Wok Stir-Fried Ono and Hawaiian Hot Peppers	Gallo Sonoma Laguna Ranch Chardonnay
Stir-Fried Curried Scallops	Turning Leaf Zinfandel/ Turning Leaf Sonoma Reserve Chardonnay
KE KAPUAHI KO'ALA (GRILL)	
Patti "O" Short Ribs	Gossamer Bay Zinfandel
Hoisin Pulehu Pork Chops	Gossamer Bay Zinfandel
Tailgate Teri Steaks	Turning Leaf Cabernet
Hilo Mango-Liliko'i-Basil Barbecue Shrimp	Turning Leaf Sonoma Reserve Chardonnay
Backyard-Style Barbecue Ribs	Turning Leaf Sonoma Reserve Pinot Noir
Swordfish, Mango and Garlic Bread Kebabs	Anapamu Chardonnay
Kona Cuisine Seafood Brochette	Gossamer Bay Chardonnay
Barbecue Beef Short Ribs	Turning Leaf Cabernet
Tailgate Annie Barbecue Leg of Lamb	Gallo Sonoma Frei Ranch Zinfandel
Sweet-Bread Variations for the Grill	Turning Leaf Chardonnay
Grilled Quesadilla Variations	Turning Leaf Chardonnay

Recipe	Recommended Choice	Recipe	Recommended Choice
Na ʻOno ʻOneʻi (Local Flavors)		**Ka Iʻa (Fish)**	
Dad's First Cooking Lesson—Steamed Moi with Lup Cheong, Green Onion and Ginger	Gossamer Bay Sauvignon Blanc	Baked Teriyaki Mahimahi	Zabaco Sauvignon Blanc
Chicken Luʻau—My Mother's Favorite	Gossamer Bay Chardonnay	Crusted Ono as Featured at Sam Choy's Restaurant	Gallo Sonoma Laguna Ranch Chardonnay
Easter Roast Lamb	Zabaco Pinot Noir/ Gallo Sonoma Frei Ranch Zinfandel	Sautéed Opakapaka with Spinach Coconut Luau Sauce	Zabaco Sauvignon Blanc
Christopher's Stir-Fried Chicken	Turning Leaf Chardonnay	Baked Whole Opakapaka with Coconut Milk	Turning Leaf Sonoma Reserve Chardonnay
Beef Luʻau Stew	Gallo Sonoma Frei Ranch Zinfandel/ Anapamu Pinot Noir	Seared Nihoa Opah	Gossamer Bay Chardonnay
Pork Luʻau Stew	Turning Leaf Sonoma Reserve Pinot Noir	Opah Macadamia Nori with Dill Cream Sauce	Turning Leaf Sonoma Reserve Pinot Noir
Honomalino Lamb with Satay Sauce	Anapamu Pinot Noir/ Zabaco Zinfandel	Blackened Ehu with Tropical Salsa	Gallo Sonoma Laguna Ranch Chardonnay
North Shore Ham Hocks with Mongo Beans and Eggplant	Zabaco Zinfandel	Stuffed ʻAhi with Hana Butter and Papaya Coulis	Gossamer Bay Chardonnay
Easy Holiday Pork Chop and Potato Scallop	Turning Leaf Sonoma Reserve Zinfandel	Pan-Fried Catfish with Sam's Sweet & Sour Sauce	Gallo Sonoma Frei Ranch Merlot
Kaʻu Mac Nut-Crusted Roast Loin of Pork with Tropical Marmalade	Gallo Sonoma Laguna Ranch Chardonnay	Poached Uku with Hollandaise and Poha Berry Sauce	Zabaco Sauvignon Blanc
Local Boy Smoked Pork	Zabaco Sauvignon Blanc	Crispy Fish with Sam Choy's Bottled Island-Style Sweet & Sour Sauce	Gossamer Bay Sauvignon Blanc
Grandma's Meatloaf	Gallo Sonoma Merlot/ Anapamu Pinot Noir		
		Ka Iʻa Pupu (Shellfish)	
Ka Moa (Chicken)		Shrimp Curry with Coconut Milk and Sugar Snap Peas	Gallo Sonoma Laguna Ranch Chardonnay
Quick and Easy Shoyu Chicken	Zabaco Zinfandel/ Turning Leaf Sonoma Reserve Pinot Noir	Stir-Fried U-10 Shrimps and Fresh Asparagus	Zabaco Sauvignon Blanc
Hibachi Miso Chicken with Peanut Butter	Turning Leaf Sonoma Reserve Chardonnay	Baked Scallops Au Gratin with Fresh Asparagus	Gallo Sonoma Frei Ranch Zinfandel
Steamed Chicken with Lup Cheong	Gossamer Bay Chardonnay	Braised Colossal Shrimp with Black Bean Sauce	Anapamu Pinot Noir/ Gallo Sonoma Laguna Ranch Chardonnay
Kahuku Roast Chicken	Gallo Sonoma Laguna Ranch Chardonnay	Baked Coconut Shrimp ʻAnaehoʻomalu Bay	Zabaco Pinot Noir
Island-Style Barbecue Cornish Game Hens	Gallo Sonoma Stefani Ranch Chardonnay	Stir-Fried Lobster and Tomatoes with Black Beans	Gossamer Bay White Zinfandel
Chicken and Portuguese Sausage Kebobs	Zabaco Zinfandel	Smoked Shrimp with Mango Salsa	Anapamu Chardonnay
Macadamia Nut Chicken Breast with Tropical Marmalade	Anapamu Chardonnay	Tomato Crab	Turning Leaf Merlot
Chicken Braised with Lily Buds and Shiitake Mushrooms	Gallo Sonoma Frei Ranch Merlot	**ʻAina Kepani (Sam in Japan)**	
		Teriyaki Squid Tokyo Style	Anapamu Pinot Noir/ Turning Leaf Sonoma Reserve Chardonnay
Stir-Fried Chicken or Beef Fajitas	Anapamu Chardonnay	Simmer Shoyu Sugar Butterfish with Vegetables	Turning Leaf Merlot
Breast of Chicken with Shiitake Sherried Butter Sauce	Gallo Sonoma Laguna Ranch Chardonnay	Baked Teriyaki Butterfish with Tofu	Turning Leaf Fume Blanc
Upcountry Sausage "Stuff It" Chicken	Gallo Sonoma Stefani Ranch Chardonnay	The All-in-One-Pot Dinner—"The Nabe"	Gossamer Bay Chardonnay

PROP DESCRIPTIONS

Page 4 — Kupe'e, an edible shellfish (Nerita polita), provided the shells for the napkin ring. Ancient Hawaiians reserved the rarest kupe'e for use by the chiefs.

Page 12 — A koa wood plate is partially shown at top left. Koa is the largest forest tree (Acacia koa) native to Hawai'i. Its valuable lumber has been used to make canoes, surfboards, calabashes, furniture and ukuleles.

Pineapple salt and pepper shakers are vintage collectibles.

Lauhala (pandanus) grown on the Big Island was used for the woven mat in the background.

Page 9 — The petroglyph turtle plate was inspired by petroglyphs, or prehistoric stone carvings, evident in places such as the lava fields of Puako, Big Island.

Page 26 — Poho kukui (kukui lamp) is a carved-stone "candleholder" for ignited nuts of the kukui (candlenut) tree. In ancient Hawai'i, kukui provided lamp oil, medicines, ornamental lei and 'inamona — a salted paste used for flavoring. The kukui is also a symbol of enlightenment.

Page 29 — Luhe'e — an octopus lure made from a large cowrie shell — is partially shown at bottom left in photo.

Naupaka, shown at upper right, is a native shrub that grows in mountains and on beaches. A legend explaining the physical separation of the shrub's two habitats tells of separated lovers. The naupaka's half flowers represent the agonies of a youth blooming in the uplands and a maiden blossoming by the sea.

Page 35 — 'Opihi (edible limpet) is a rare delicacy savored at Hawaiian feasts. The shelled meat sells for more than

$100 a gallon. Polished 'opihi shells are shown at left, while raw 'opihi still in the shell garnishes the poke.

A milo wood bowl is shown. Hawaiians make food bowls out of milo, kamani and kou wood because these woods keep food without changing its flavors.

Page 42 — "Laua'e" bowl was inspired by the fragrant laua'e fern, which has been likened to a sweet loved one or to cherished memories.

Page 44 — This lei is made of 'a'ali'i (Dodonaea) that blooms in the summer on Moloka'i island.

Page 49 — A handmade throwing fishnet, a Choy family heirloom, is pictured in the background.

Page 52 — A contemporary stylized chief's food bowl is made of kamani wood.

Kapa (tapa), shown in background, is a 19th-century kapa passed down through the Papa family of the Big Island. Earlier Hawaiians made kapa by pounding tree barks, printing designs with plant dyes and making them into clothing or blankets.

Lei hulu, or red feather lei, has a carved-wood niho palaoa — a replica of a whale-tooth pendant, which is a symbol of royalty.

Page 61 — A red wiliwili seed lei is pictured at right.

Page 79 — The lei wili shown is made by winding together fresh or dried flowers, ferns and leaves.

Page 90 — Lei pupu Ni'ihau is a lei of rare and expensive Ni'ihau shells. The lei, shown at top left, is less than a yard long and costs $4,000. Residents of the private island of Ni'ihau painstakingly collect the tiny shells — many smaller than rice grains — and string them by hand.

Page 97 — This lei wili was made by winding together 'a'ali'i, bozu, kangaroo paws, likolehua and palapalai fern.

Page 100 — Vintage fabric dates from the early 1950s.

Page 106 — Palaka, or block-print cloth, dates from early plantation days in Hawai'i. Paniolo (cowboy) spurs, ropes and barbecue beef point to Parker Ranch's legacy and continuing role in Hawai'i's cattle ranching industry.

Page 112 —This lei of pansies — as well as the grass-fed beef pictured — is associated with the 164-year tradition of paniolos (cowboys) and women of Waimea, Big Island.

Page 121 — Lei hulu (feather lei) serves as a brilliant blue hat band. The ancient Hawaiians were conservationists; when they were doing featherwork, they would pluck only two or three feathers at a time from a bird, then let it go.

Page 124 — Ipu heke (gourd drum with a top section) is used as a drum to accompany chants and hula.

Lei 'akulikuli features brilliant pink, rose and orange flowers of the ice plant, which originated in Africa and is raised in the cool uplands of Waimea, Big Island.

Page 149 — This seed lei was made with the seeds of kukui, plumeria (frangipani) and wiliwili.

Page 188 — The seed lei at upper left was made of Manila palm seeds and false wiliwili seeds.

ARTISTS' CREDITS

Page 4 — Kupe'e necklace by Belinda Pali.

Page 12 — Koa butter dish by master woodcarver Dan De Luz of Woods Inc., Hilo and Waimea, Big Island.
Vintage pineapple salt and pepper shakers courtesy of Paul Hirata of Honolulu.

Page 9 — Turtle plate by Gary Wagner of Puako, Big Island.

Page 26 — Poho kukui (kukui lamps) and stone bowls by stone carver Craig White of Waimea, Big Island.

Page 29 — Avocado wood bowl and luhe'e (octopus lure) from the extensive collection by Dan De Luz.

Page 35 — Milo wood bowl by Dan De Luz.

Page 42 — "Laua'e" ceramic platter by Sandy Sater of Kona, Big Island.

Page 44 — Petroglyph etched-glass bowl and candleholders by Gary Wagner.
Lei by Marie McDonald.

Page 49 — Throw net was handmade by the late Felix Joyce, father-in-law of chef Sam Choy.

Page 52 — Chief's food bowl by stone/woodcarver Tom Pico.
Kapa courtesy of Jennifer and Corky Bryan of Waimea, Big Island.
Feather lei by Carol Tanabe.

Page 61 — Norfolk pine wood platter by woodworker Kelly Dunn of Kohala, Big Island.
Lei by seed leimaker David Aguiar of the Big Island.

Page 68 — Glass platters by Babs Miyano of Honolulu
Etched-glass lantern by Joe Rivera of Honoka'a, Big Island.
Hand-dyed sarong by Rochelle Wolfe of Sea Maiden of Hawai'i, Big Island.

Page 73 — "Ki'i" sculptures in alabaster and other stone, by sculptor Sara Lawless of the Big Island.

Page 79 — Lei wili by Amy Rosato.
Petroglyph-print silk scarf by Junko Weeks of Hilo, Big Island.

Page 90 — Curly koa chopsticks by Chris Allen of Volcano area, Big Island.

Page 82 — Jade turtle pendant by fisherman/carver Louis the Fisher.

Page 97 — Lei by Marie McDonald.

Page 100 — Koa ukulele by Konawaena High School student Jimmy Bustu; instructor Guy Sasaki.
Vintage fabric by Locals Only.

Page 112 — Lei by Marie McDonald.

Page 116 — Ti-leaf plate of Hamakua Clay Co.
Fish etched-glass bricks by Joe Rivera.
Ti-leaf lei by Amy Rosato.

Page 121 — Ceramic platter by Julie Warner of Puako, Big Island.
Lei hulu (feather lei) by Moana Wai Lin Choy, sister of chef Sam Choy.

Page 124 — Ipu heke by Keali'i T.M. Lum, Kamehameha Schools graduate who is attending the University of San Francisco on a baseball scholarship.
Ipu grown by farmer/artisan Calvin Hoe of Hakipu'u, O'ahu.

Lei by master leimaker Marie McDonald of Waimea, Big Island. She is the author of "Ka Lei — The Leis of Hawai'i" and a former recipient of a National Endowment of the Arts fellowship.

Page 130 — Hand-dyed sarong by Rochelle Wolfe.

Page 138 — Koa tongs by woodcarver Dan Lappala of Laupahoehoe, Big Island.

Page 149 — Seed lei by James Key.

Page 157 — Raku sushi plate by Julie Warner.
Raku bowls by Miles Thurlby.

Page 160 — Carved stone bowl by Craig White.

Page 168 — Hand-dyed fabric by Rochelle Wolfe.

Page 176 — Bowl by Dan De Luz.

Page 180 — Ceramic bowl by potter/art teacher Edmund Enomoto of Honolulu.

Page 185 — Ceramic bowl by Edmund Enomoto.

Page 188 — Ceramic slab bowls by Edmund Enomoto.
Lei by David Aguiar.

'Ahi — Hawaiian name for yellowfin tuna.

Aku — Hawaiian name for skipjack tuna.

Asian eggplant — long, slender eggplant with purple, lavender or green-colored skin.

Bean sprouts — fresh sprouts of the green mung bean.

Big Island — called Hawai'i (besides the state); the largest island in the Hawaiian Islands.

Black beans — Chinese fermented and often salted soybeans used as a flavoring; can (but don't need to) be soaked in water to remove some saltiness.

Carpaccio — Italian word for raw fish preparations.

Chinese five-spice powder — pungent spicing mixture of Sichuan peppercorn, cinnamon, cloves, fennel seed and star anise.

Cilantro — Chinese parsley.

Coconut milk — rich, creamy liquid squeezed from grated coconut; can use fresh, canned and frozen.

Daikon — Asian radish; a long, off-white tuber with white flesh.

Furikake — Japanese condiment of dried seaweed flakes and sesame seeds, available in the Asian section of markets.

Ginger — spicy, pungent rhizome.

Gon lo mein — Chinese fried noodle.

Hawaiian red chile pepper — small, potently hot chile pepper grown and used widely in Hawai'i.

Hawaiian salt — white or pink coarse sea salt traditionally harvested on Kaua'i island.

Hawaiian sweet bread — See: Portuguese sweet bread.

Hibachi — small, portable, inexpensive Japanese outdoor grill used widely in back yards, on patios and at beaches in Hawai'i.

Ho'i'o — Hawaiian name for edible fern shoots.

Hoisin sauce — spicy-sweet Chinese product used for flavoring; incorporates soybeans, garlic and chile pepper.

'Inamona — traditional Hawaiian condiment made of roasted, ground and salted kukui nut meat; used to flavor poke.

Jicama — crunchy root vegetable that is eaten raw or cooked.

Kajiki — Japanese name for Pacific blue marlin fish.

Kamado — Trademark of a Japanese-style covered grill.

Kiawe — Hawaiian name for the algaroba tree, whose wood and chips are used for barbecuing and smoking.

Kim chee — hot, spicy Korean pickled vegetables, usually Napa cabbage or cucumbers preserved in a brine of salt, garlic and chile peppers.

Kukui — refers to the candlenut tree and its nuts (see: 'Inamona)

Light chicken stock — fat-free, reduced-sodium chicken stock.

Light soy sauce — reduced-sodium soy sauce.

Liliko'i — Hawaiian name for passion fruit, a shiny yellow or purple egg-shaped fruit whose tart, sweetly fragrant pulp is strained and used in sauces, sorbets and pastries.

Lily buds — dried buds of a certain day lily, available in Chinese groceries.

Limu — Hawaiian word for seaweed.

Lollo rosa — curly red lettuce of Italian origin.

Lu'au — young taro leaves; cook thoroughly 50 to 60 minutes before eating; used in laulau; has come to mean a "feast" where laulau is traditionally served.

Lup cheong — Chinese dried sausage.

Lychee — sweetly fragrant, inch-round fruits from the tropical lychee tree; fruit available fresh or canned in Asian section of markets.

Macadamia nuts — round, oily nut with a creamy, slightly crunchy texture; grows on trees mostly on the Big Island.

Mahimahi — Hawaiian name for dolphinfish.

Mango — oval tropical fruit with golden-orange flesh and an enticing, aromatic flavor; skin color ranges from yellow-orange to burgundy to green; from a quarter-pound up in size; available in the produce section of markets; can substitute peaches or nectarines in recipes.

Mirin — glutinous rice wine that adds sweetness; available in the Asian section of markets.

Miso — fermented soybean paste.

Mochi — glutinous rice.

Mochiko — glutinous rice flour.

Monchong — big-scale pomfret.

Mongo beans — split dried mung beans.

Nairagi — Japanese name for striped marlin.

Nori — Japanese word for paper-thin sheets of dried seaweed; used to wrap roll sushi; available in the Asian section of markets.

Ogo — Japanese name for Gracilaria seaweed.

Onaga — Hawaiian name for red snapper

Ono — Hawaiian name for long ocean fish in the mackerel family; also known as wahoo.

Opah — Hawaiian name for moonfish.

Opakapaka — Hawaiian name for pink or ruby snapper.

Opihi — limpet that is eaten raw; grows on rocks, often in high-wave areas; the fresh or prefrozen delicacy is prized at feasts.

Oyster sauce — popular Asian seasoning consisting of oysters, brine and soy sauce.

Panko — Japanese-style fine bread crumbs; can substitute Italian bread crumbs.

Papaya — melon-like fruit with a smooth, yellow or orange flesh and a shiny green skin, usually about a pound in size; available in the produce section of markets.

Passion fruit — See: Liliko'i.

Poha — yellow, cherry-size fruit with a spicy pulp and lantern-like parchment covering; rare in Hawai'i; known elsewhere as cape gooseberry, ground cherry, or husk tomato.

Poke — Hawaiian word for "slice"; refers to a traditional Hawaiian dish of sliced raw seafood, fresh seaweed, Hawaiian salt and Hawaiian red chile peppers.

Portuguese sweet bread — sweet egg bread, also known as Hawaiian sweet bread or Easter bread.

Portuguese sausage — a popular meaty product with mild, medium, or hot spicing; substitute Italian sausage.

Red chile (pepper) paste — commercial preparation made of red chile peppers and sometimes garlic; available in the Asian section of markets.

Rice vinegar — colorless Japanese vinegar used in sushi; available in the Asian section of markets.

Rice wine — See: Mirin.

Sake — yellowish, slightly sweet rice wine.

Sashimi — traditional Japanese appetizer of sliced raw fish.

Sesame oil — dense, flavorful oil from the sesame seed; used widely in Asian cookery; use sparingly in cooked preparations, such as marinades, or in fresh preparations, such as poke.

Shiitake mushrooms — meaty, full-bodied mushrooms originally from Japan and Korea, and now cultivated in a number of U.S. states; used fresh or dried.

Shiso — Japanese word for the edible beefsteak plant; this purple- or green-colored Asian herb of the mint family has tones of mint, basil, tarragon, cilantro, cinnamon and anise.

Shoyu — See: Soy Sauce.

Shutome — Japanese name for swordfish.

Soy sauce — very important Asian flavoring made of fermented soy beans.

Spiny lobster — clawless blue lobster found in Hawaiian waters; substitute Maine or other lobster.

Star anise — star-shaped, dark-brown pod that is a common Chinese spicing.

Sugar snap peas — delightfully sweet pea, which is a cross between the English pea and the Chinese snow pea.

Taro — nutritious, starchy tuber used for making poi, the staple of the traditional Hawaiian diet; more than 200 taro varieties are grown worldwide; steam, boil or bake taro thoroughly 20 to 90 minutes, depending on size.

Taro bread — yeast or quick bread with cooked, mashed taro in the dough.

Teriyaki — Japanese sauce or marinade with soy sauce, sugar and fresh ginger.

Thick soy sauce — dark soy sauce.

Tofu — fresh soybean curd; bland and therefore versatile.

Uku — Hawaiian name for gray snapper.

Wasabi — Japanese version of horseradish; pungent condiment.

Wok — versatile round-bottomed pan universal in Chinese cookery; used with and without a cover for stir-frying, steaming, boiling, braising and deep-frying.

Won bok — Chinese cabbage or Napa cabbage.

SAM CHOY

From the seacoast resort town of Kona, on the Big Island of Hawai'i, Chef Sam Choy presides over an international whirl of culinary activities. They include the spring 1996 opening of Sam Choy's Tokyo restaurant; his headlining of a culinary cruise from Vancouver to Alaska through the Inside Passage; and his nomination as 1995 James Beard Foundation Northwest Chef of the Year.

Big Island Mayor Stephen Yamashiro proclaimed Chef Choy the Culinary Ambassador of the Big Island. He also was named to "Hawai'i's Fastest 50" — an echelon of the State's fastest-growing private small businesses. And, he hosts the weekly "In the Kitchen with Sam Choy" cooking show.

The lively pace continues with the release of his third cookbook, *The Choy of Cooking*, released one year after his best-selling *With Sam Choy — Cooking from the Heart*. The Hawai'i State House of Representatives saluted him with a certificate for Best Big Island Restaurant of 1995. And, he recently unveiled a signature line of sauces and dressings.

It all started in another seacoast town where 44-year-old Sam Choy was raised — in La'ie on the Hawaiian island of O'ahu. He learned cooking basics in the family lu'au-catering business and restaurant. He refined those skills while earning a food service degree at Kapi'olani Community College.

He went on to serve as executive sous chef at the Hyatt Kuilima Hotel; chef at the Oscar Restaurant in the Waldorf-Astoria Hotel; and executive chef at the Kona Hilton Beach & Tennis Resort.

He opened his flagship Sam Choy's Restaurant in Kona in 1991 and the upscale Sam Choy's Diamond Head restaurant near Waikiki in 1995.

He is the only Hawai'i-born chef among the original exponents of Hawai'i Regional Cuisine, so he gives a unique homegrown spin to the movement's emphasis on fresh island products and classic Pacific stylings.

"Home-cooked meals are my personal favorite," he says. "Most people would have to agree that their favorite foods are the ones mom or dad would make for them at home. It's what people refer to as comfort foods. They bring happy memories back to us when we eat them. This is why I believe so strongly in catering to the family. It makes me feel good when I see a family come into my restaurant, not only to enjoy my food but, more importantly, each other's company and fellowship."

Chef Choy lives with his family — wife Carol Greene Choy and sons Sam Jr., 16, and Christopher, 11 — in that seacoast town of Kona.

BIOGRAPHIES

JOANNIE DOBBS *graduated in dietetics from Michigan State University and holds a Ph.D. in nutrition from the University of California at Davis. She is a Certified Nutrition Specialist (C.N.S.) who has worked in food and nutrition for more than 25 years. As sole proprietor of Exploring New Concepts, Dobbs is a consultant to restaurant chefs and food companies, and does nutrient analyses for various publications. She is co-author of the recent cookbook,* Bone Appetit, *developed for the Hawai'i Osteoporosis Foundation. She is also a member of the American Culinary Federation's Chef de Cuisine Organization, Hawai'i Chapter.*

CATHERINE KEKOA ENOMOTO *is a 14-year staff writer, food columnist and copy editor with the* Honolulu Star-Bulletin. *She was a contributing writer to the book,* Notable Women of Hawai'i. *She graduated from the Kamehameha Schools and Beloit College in Beloit, Wisconsin, and holds a master of journalism degree from the University of California at Berkeley.*

LEO GONZALEZ *has art directed and designed more than 20 books about Hawai'i for Mutual Publishing, winning numerous awards, including the prestigious NY Art Directors Club,* Print's Regional Design Annuals *and* The Pele Awards. *His studio, Gonzalez Design Company, designs annual reports, brochures and logos for a range of corporate, institutional and individual clients. Born in Manila, raised in Manoa and lived in Manhattan, he now resides in Aina Haina with his wife Phyllis and sons Matthew and Marcus.*

FAITH OGAWA *is chef/consultant to the nutritional service department of North Hawai'i Community Hospital, a progressive, state-of-the-art facility that honors complementary healing techniques. She specializes in "healthful cuisine with the spirit of aloha." Ogawa also is involved in food and beverage sales and marketing, and food styling out of Waimea, Big Island, where she lives with her 11-year-old son, Kahlil Dean. Formerly, she served as restaurant chef at Mauna Lani Bay Hotel and Bungalows, and food service instructor at Kapi'olani Community College. She holds a food service degree from Leeward Community College. She was also the food and prop stylist for* With Sam Choy: Cooking from the Heart.

DOUGLAS PEEBLES *has photographed a number of books on Hawai'i, including eight for Mutual Publishing —* From the Skies of Paradise Series, Landmark Hawai'i *and* Hawai'i: A Floral Paradise. The Choy of Cooking *is his second cookbook project. His newspaper and magazine credits include the* New York Times, Los Angeles Times, National Geographic, Conde-Naste Traveler, *and* Travel Holiday. *Peebles is originally from Jacksonville, Florida, and has lived in Hawai'i for 22 years. He, wife Margaret, sons Brad and Kevin, and two dogs live in Kailua, O'ahu.*

Left to right: Leo Gonzalez, Catherine Kekoa Enomoto, Faith Ogawa, Joannie Dobbs and Douglas Peebles

Aeder, Kirk Lee—ii
Ah Hoy, George—67
'ahi (yellowfin tuna)—4, 14, 17, 25, 27, 30, 31, 33, 96, 169, 184
'Ahi and Shrimp Candy—17
'Ahi Poke Salad—33
Akebono (Rowan, Chad)—199, 202
aku—25, 27, 30
Aku Poke—30
All-In-One Pot Dinner-the "Nabe," The—201
'Anaeho'omalu Bay—187
arugula—51
asparagus—181, 182

Backyard Barbecue Sauce—111
Backyard-Style Barbecue Ribs—102
bacon—14, 105
bake—120, 129, 133, 151, 155, 156, 161, 169, 182, 187, 200, 207, 209, 211
Baked Coconut Shrimp 'Anaeho'omalu Bay—187
Baked Scallops Au Gratin with Fresh Asparagus—182
Baked Teriyaki Butterfish with Tofu—200
Baked Teriyaki Mahimahi—155
Baked Whole Opakapaka with Coconut Milk—161
banana liqueur—216
bananas—45, 109, 211, 216, 217
Barbecue Beef Short Ribs—107
barley—15
basting mixture—136
Beef or Pork Lu'au Stew—123
bean sprouts—18, 201
béarnaise—8, 21
beef—67, 95, 107, 115, 123, 133, 148
beef brisket—123
beef short ribs—95, 107
beef stew—67
beef tenderloin fillets—115
beer—7, 36, 139
bell peppers—43, 51, 78, 86, 88, 122, 148, 167, 171, 175, 191
bell peppers, roasting—51, 86
Bella Mushroom Salad—51
Best Crabmeat Soup with Taro—19
Big Brothers/Big Sisters of Honolulu—85
black beans—181, 186, 189
black bean sauce—60, 81
Blackened Ehu with Tropical Salsa—167
Blue Pincers Poke—37
blue crab—37
bluefin tuna—163
bonus dessert tip (vanilla sauce), cooking tip—209
Boston chowder, Manhattan-style—14
Braised Colossal Shrimp with Black Bean Sauce—186
Braised Ginger Honey Chicken—70
braised—62, 65, 70, 162, 186
bread crumbs—25, 182
bread pudding—209
breadfruit—41

bread—211
Breast of Chicken with Shiitake Sherried Butter Sauce—150
broccoli—148, 171
brochettes—105
broil—51, 86, 96, 99, 125, 195
butter, "Da Hana" flavored—170
butter, garlic—109
butter, ginger-cilantro—109
butterfish (black cod)—198, 200
buttermilk—128, 182

Cabbage—18, 155, 196
Canadian bacon—13
cape gooseberries—20, 45, 47, 173
cape gooseberry jelly—131
carpaccio—196
carrots—148, 211
cashew nuts—27
casserole—110
"chanko nabe"—199
Chardonnay—59
cheddar cheese—110
cheese—8, 15, 51, 110, 182, 187
Chicken and Portuguese Sausage Kebabs—144
Chicken Braised with Lily Buds and Shiitake Mushrooms—147
Chicken Lu'au-My Mother's Favorite—118
chicken Kiev—169
chicken stir-fry—v
chicken—7, 10, 18, 45, 62, 65, 66, 70, 71, 78, 80, 81, 118, 122, 126, 133, 136, 137, 139, 140, 141, 144, 146, 147, 148, 150, 151
children, cooking with—103, 122
chile paste—20, 28
chile pepper water—110, 123
chile peppers—80, 86, 88, 184
chile-garlic sauce—125
Chinese cabbage—63
Chinese five-spice powder—17, 96, 98, 137
Chinese snow peas—122
Chocolate Macadamia Cream Cheese Pie—210
chocolate chip—109
chocolate—210
chop, julienne, mince, cooking tips—41
chowder—14
Choy, Carol—v, 206
Choy, Christopher—v, 24, 122
Choy, Clairemoana Meyer (mom)—v, 118, 133, 215
Choy, Hung Sam (dad)—v, 58, 215
Choy, Moana Wai Lin—v
Choy, Patrick Wing Hing—v, 214, 216, 217
Choy, Sam Jr.—v, 24, 30, 148, 202
Choy, Sam—224
Choy, Wai Sun—v, 210
Christopher's Stir-Fried Chicken—122
chutney—6, 20
cioppino—184
clam juice—184
clam stock—59, 201

clams—60, 184
clarifying butter—21
coconut milk, making fresh, cooking tip—179
coconut milk—vi, 8, 19, 118, 125, 129, 159, 161, 179, 207
coconut—99, 187, 207, 211, 217
Cold Chicken Tossed with Fresh Ginger Pesto—71
Columbia Basin Junior College—215
comfort foods—66, 224
cooking tips—3, 27, 36, 41, 98, 179, 209
Cool Summer Night Cioppino—184
Cornish game hens—142
corn—50
coulis—170
Crab and Shrimp Stuffed Shiitake Mushrooms with Béarnaise Sauce—8
crabmeat—8, 19, 41, 50
crabs, how to clean—37
crab—8, 37, 191
cracker crumbs—8
Crawfish Country, vignette—183
crawfish—183
cream cheese—210
cream—8, 14, 19, 133, 159, 162, 175, 179, 182, 209
Crispy Fish with Sam Choy's Bottled Island-Style Sweet & Sour Sauce—174
Crusted Ono as Featured at Sam Choy's Restaurants—156
cucumber—36
curried—89
curry—179
cuttlefish—195

"**D**a Hana Butter"—170
Da Wife's Bean Soup—13
Dad's First Cooking Lesson-Steamed Moi with Lup Cheong, Green Onion & Ginger—117
Daiba—127
Daiki (Kipapa, Percy)—202
daikon (Asian radish)—196, 201
dashi konbu—201
dashi-no-moto—201
Datta, Tane and Vicki—47
Death by Chocolate—210
Decade of the Chef, vignette—85
Deep-Fried Mahimahi Macadamia Nut Fingers—3
deep-frying—3, 10, 53, 83, 169, 174
Definitely Easy Deboned Shoyu Chicken Drumettes—18
Deglazing Grace, vignette—67
deglazing—67
desserts—206, 207, 209, 210, 211, 212, 214, 216, 217
Dill Cream Sauce—175
Dill Vinaigrette—54
dill—8, 54, 156, 166, 175, 187
Dobbs, Joannie—vii, 225
Domenico, Nick—103
dressing, Hilo Tropical Fruit Slaw—45

dressing, miso—55
dressing, Puna Papaya and Maui Onion—54
dressing, tomato—51
"dry" marinade—94

Easter Roast Lamb—119
Easter—119
Easy Holiday Pork Chop and Potato Scallop—128
Easy Local Ribs—120
eggplant—80, 91, 126
eggs—50
ehu (orange snapper)—167
Emu vs. Imu, vignette—145
enokitake mushrooms—201
Enomoto, Catherine—225

Fajitas—148
farmer Ben—47
filleting fish, cooking tip—27
filleting—27, 31
Fish Stock—21
fish cake—201
fish odor, how to remove from hands—31
fish stock—14, 21, 162
fish—3, 4, 17, 21, 25, 27, 30, 33, 43, 53, 88, 96, 104, 117, 154, 155, 156, 158, 159, 160, 169, 162, 163, 164, 166, 167, 171, 172, 174, 184, 196, 198, 200, 201
500 'Ahi, vignette—31
flambé—216
French toast—109, 211
fruit—6, 20, 21, 40, 43, 45, 47, 84, 99, 101, 104, 105, 110, 111, 120, 129, 131, 133, 144, 158, 167, 170, 173, 175, 190, 206, 207, 211, 212, 214, 216, 217
fry fillets—158
furikake—110
fusille—43

Gallo wines—16, 17, 28, 53, 59, 68, 79, 87, 91, 95, 96, 115, 121, 141, 161, 174, 179, 185, 195, 196, 218-219
Garlic Shrimp with Spinach, Red Peppers & Oyster Mushrooms—86
garlic-chile sauce—91
Ginger Clams with Black Bean Sauce—60
Ginger Shoyu Pork—63
Ginger, Ginger Steamed Mussels—59
Gingered Lobster—72
Gingered Scallops with Colorful Soba Noodles—69
glaze—133
goatfish—163
gon lo mein (Chinese fried noodles)—v
Gonzalez, Leo—225
Goto, Aisake—203
Goto, Hitoshi—127, 203
Grandma's Meatloaf—133
Grilled Quesadilla Variations—110
Grilled Tropical Fruits—217
grilling vegetables—94

grill—7, 94, 96, 139, 142, 144, 150, 195, 214, 216
grouper—105
guava jam—109, 110
guava-nectar concentrate—212
guava—214

Half-and-half—14, 159, 162
halibut—105, 117
ham hocks—13, 126
ham leg—120
ham shanks—13
hapu'upu'u (grouper or sea bass)—105
haupia—206, 207
Helena Pali Opihi Limu Poke—34
herbs—156, 166, 187
Hibachi Bananas Foster—216
Hibachi Miso Chicken with Peanut Butter—139
Hibachi Pineapple Spears—214
Hilo Haupia Squares—207
Hilo Mano-Liliko'i-Basil Barbecue Shrimp—101
Hilo Open Market—45
Hilo Tropical Fruit Slaw—45
Hilo—45, 101, 171, 207
Hoe, Arline—67
Hoisin Pulehu Pork Chops—98
hoisin sauce—98, 125, 148
Hollandaise Sauce—173
Honaunau Market—47
honey—45, 70, 108, 111, 136, 141, 151, 167
Honomalino Lamb with Satay Sauce—125
horseradish—4, 20
Hukilau Bay—27
Hulihe'e Palace—2

Ice cream—209, 216, 217
'Inamona (kukui nut paste)—24, 27
Island-Style Barbecue Cornish Game Hens—142
Italian sausage—11

Jalapeno peppers—110
James Beard House—85
Japanese work ethic, manners—127
Japan—127, 154, 163, 183, 194, 202
jicama—196

Ka'u Mac Nut-Crusted Roast Loin of Pork with Tropical Marmalade—131
Kahawai'i, Robert Mona—117, 199
Kahuku Roast Chicken—141
Kahuku—126, 141
kalua pig—110, 145
kamado grill—139
Kamuela Dry-Rub Tenderloin—115
Kamuela—115
Kapi'olani Community College—67, 178, 215
Katase, Steve—55
Keahole Ogo Salad with Miso Dressing—55
Keahole—55, 72

kebabs—17, 101, 104, 144
kiawe wood—96, 190
kim-chee—37
kiwi—45
knives—31
Kobayashi, Isamu—ii
kochu jang—28
Kona Cuisine Seafood Brochettes—105
Kona Cuisine—105
Kona mushroom—86
Kona Seafood Chowder—14
Konishiki (Atisanoe, Salevaa)—103, 199, 203
Korean-Style Tako Poke—28
Koryu (Cosier, Eric)—202
kukui lamp—27
kukui nuts—27
kulolo—206

Lamb Salad—46
lamb—46, 108, 119, 125
liliko'i—101
liliko'i concentrate—101
lily buds—147
lime—96
limu—34, 55
Limu Lomilomi Relish—55
limu kohu (seaweed)—27, 30
limu manauea (seaweed)—30
lipoa (seaweed)—30
lobster—72, 77, 184, 189
Local Boy Smoked Pork—132
Local flavors—114
Local-Style Ginger Braised Chicken—62
lollo rosa—51
Lomilomi Salmon with a Twist—53
long rice—201
Louisiana—145, 183
low fat—vi, vii, 7, 15, 41, 50, 54, 62, 70, 72, 78, 84, 91, 122, 126, 129, 141, 147, 148,   175, 189, 191, 195, 214
low-fat recipes, "The Old Sand Island Days"
    Ogo Pickle-"Not"—48
    Ahi and Shrimp Candy—17
    Aku Poke—30
    All-In-One Pot Dinner-the "Nabe," The—201
    Backyard Barbecue Sauce—111
    Baked Teriyaki Mahimahi—155
    Bella Mushroom Salad—51
    Cool Summer Night Cioppino—184
    Gingered Scallops with Colorful Soba Noodles—69
    Grilled Tropical Fruits—217
    Helena Pali Opihi Limu Poke—34
    Hilo Mango-Liliko'i-Basil Barbecue Shrimp—101
    Hilo Tropical Fruit Slaw—45
    Keahole Ogo Salad with Miso Dressing—55
    Limu Lomilomi Relish—55
    Lychee Oh Lychee Monchong—158
    Mango Guava Sorbet—212
    Mango Salsa—190
    Papaya Coulis—170

Papaya-Mango Salsa—175
Pepper-Papaya–Pineapple Chutney—20
Poha Berry Sauce—173
Smoked Shrimp with Mango Salsa—190
Stir Fried U-10 Shrimps and Fresh Asparagus—181
Summer 'Ahi Tartare—4
Tailgate Teri Sauce—111
Tako Poke—36
Three-Fruit Sherbet—214
Tropical Marmalade—20
Tropical Salsa—167
low-fat tips—7, 15, 41, 50, 54, 62, 70, 72, 78, 84, 91, 122, 126, 129, 141, 147, 148, 175, 189, 191, 195, 214
lower-fat tips—3, 4, 6, 8, 10, 13, 14, 18, 19, 25, 33, 37, 43, 46, 53, 54, 59, 60, 63, 65, 66, 71, 77, 80, 81, 83, 86, 88, 95, 96, 98, 99, 102, 104, 105, 107, 108, 115, 117, 118, 119, 123, 125, 128, 131, 132, 133, 137, 139, 140, 142, 144, 146, 150, 151, 156, 159, 161, 162, 164, 166, 167, 169, 171, 172, 173, 174, 179, 182, 186, 187, 196, 198, 200, 207, 209, 210, 211, 216, 217
lu'au—34, 118, 123, 145, 159
lup cheong sausage—117, 140
Lychee Oh Lychee Monchong—158
lychees—45, 84, 217, 158

Ma-po tofu—80
Macadamia Nut Chicken Breast with Tropical Marmalade—146
Macadamia Nut Dried-Papaya "Always Tastes Great" Bread Pudding—209
macadamia nuts—3, 46, 71, 131, 146, 156, 167, 207, 209, 210, 211, 216
mahimahi (dolphinfish)—3, 14, 155, 158, 184
Maine lobster—72
making fresh coconut milk, cooking tip—179
mana—127
manchong—162
Mango Béarnaise Sauce—21
Mango Bread—211
Mango Guava Sorbet—212
Mango Salsa—190
mango—21, 45, 101, 104, 105, 167, 170, 175, 190, 206, 211, 212, 214, 217
marlin (kajiki, nairagi)—14, 169
Masuto, Norman—129
Matsuda, Melvin—126
Maui onion—4, 28, 41, 48, 50, 54, 55, 132, 159, 161, 162, 184
Mauna Kea—115
mayonnaise—161
McIlhenny family—183
meatballs—133
meatloaf—133
Meeker, Kevin—11, 85, 103
mince—41

mint—20, 51
mirin (sweet rice wine)—66, 146, 201
Miso Miso Boneless Chicken Thighs with Ginger—66
miso—7, 55, 66, 139, 155, 201
mochiko—10
mochi—10
moi (Pacific threadfin)—117, 154
Mom's Story: 'He Never Looked Back,' vignette—215
Monchong with Onion Compote—162
monchong (big-scale pomfret)—158, 162
mongo beans—126
Mother Goose Farms, Honolulu—146
mozzarella cheese—110
Musashimaru (Penitani, Fiamalu)—199, 202
mushrooms—8, 25, 43, 51, 86, 147, 150, 164, 191, 201
mussels—43, 59, 184
mustard cabbage—63
mustard—4
My Friend Must Wait, vignette—127

Nanfu (Kekauoha, Kaleo)—199, 202, 203
nectarine—170
New York steaks—99
Nihoa islet—164
Nineties Style Potato Salad—50
nishime (Japanese stew)—198
noodles—33, 69
nori—166
North Shore Ham Hocks with Mongo Beans and Eggplant—126
North Shore—126
nuts—3, 27, 46, 71, 131, 146, 156, 167, 207, 209, 210, 211, 216

Octopus (tako)—28, 36
octopus, how to clean fresh—36
Ogawa, Faith—225
ogo—25, 28, 30, 33, 37, 47, 48, 53, 55
oil, hot ginger-pepper—196
oil, olive, rosemary-garlic—109
"Old Sand Island Days"
    Ogo Pickle-"Not," The—48
olives—50
onaga (red snapper)—105, 158
O'Neil, Dutch—202
onion compote—162
Ono Carpaccio with Hot Ginger Pepper Oil—196
ono (wahoo)—14, 88, 154, 156, 169, 174, 184, 196
Opah Macadamia Nori with Dill Cream Sauce—166
opah (moonfish)—43, 164, 166
opakapaka (pink snapper)—105, 154, 158, 159, 161
opihi—34
orange—43, 111, 173
orange juice, cooking tip—98
orange juice—51, 69, 105, 107, 125, 142, 144, 155

orange marmalade—171
oyster sauce—60, 78, 122, 164, 191, 210

Pacific threadfin—117
Pan-Fried Catfish with Sam's Sweet & Sour Sauce—171
Pan-Fried Spicy Eggplant—91
Panko (Japanese-style fine bread crumbs)—25
Papaya Coulis—170
Papaya-Mango Salsa—175
papaya—6, 20, 45, 54, 167, 170, 175, 209, 211
parmesan cheese—8, 15, 182, 187
passion-fruit nectar concentrate—214
pasta—43
Patti "O" Short Ribs—95
peach—170
peanut butter—109, 139
Peebles, Douglas—225
Pepper-Papaya-Pineapple Chutney—20
peppercorn—110
pepper—6, 20
pesto—58, 71
Philly Steak Sand With, vignette—103
Philly steak sandwiches—103
pickle—48
pie—210
pineapple juice—84, 144, 171
pineapple rind—190
pineapple—6, 20, 45, 84, 99, 105, 110, 120, 129, 133, 144, 167, 170, 214, 217
plantations—2
plate lunch—40
plum—170
poaching—69, 71, 172, 178
Poached Uku with Hollandaise and Poha Berry Sauce—172
Poha Berry Sauce—173
poha berries—20, 45, 47, 173
poha jelly—131
Poke Patties—25
Poke Recipe Contest—24
poke—24, 85
pork chops—98, 128
pork loin—131
pork spareribs—102, 120, 123
pork—60, 63, 83, 84, 132
portobello—51
Portuguese bean soup—11
Portuguese sausage—13, 144, 151
Portuguese sweet bread—104, 109, 131, 151, 209
potatoes—13, 14, 15, 50, 107, 115, 119, 128, 172
pound cake—217
presentation—183
prosciutto—15
Prudhomme, Paul—85, 145, 183
Puna Papaya and Maui Onion Dressing—54
Puna—54
pupu—2
purple sweet potato—41

Quick and "Tastes Good" Barley Soup—15
Quick and Easy Shoyu Chicken—137

Radicchio—43, 45
radish—48
raisins—211
rambutan—45
red wine vinegar—144
relish—48, 55
rice—132, 194
rice vinegar—28, 48, 51, 54, 55, 83, 107
Richard, Chris—145
Ritz cracker—156
roast chicken—136
roast—119, 131, 141
rosemary—15, 109
Royal Hawaiian Sea Farms—55
rum—216

Sacarob, Harvey—47
sake—18, 36, 66, 155, 195, 201
salad greens—33
salmon—43, 53, 110, 117, 158, 201
salsa, mango—190
salsa, papaya-mango—175
salsa—167, 175, 190
salt, rubbing on meat or fish—107
Sam Choy's Diamond Head—76, 77
Sam Choy's Kona Cuisine Hawaiian Pineapple Barbecue Sauce—84
Sam Choy's Kona Cuisine Island Style Sweet & Sour Sauce—171, 174
Sam Choy's Restaurants—85, 156
Sam Choy's Tokyo—127, 202
Sam in Japan, vignette—199
Sam's Grandmother—v
sambal—20
Sand Island—47, 48
Satay Sauce—125
Sauce, Backyard Barbecue—111
Sauce, Barbecue—107
Sauce, Easy Local Rib—120
Sauce, Hollandaise—173
Sauce, Mango Béarnaise—21
Sauce, Poha Berry—173
Sauce, Sam's Sweet & Sour—171
Sauce, Shiitake Sherried Butter—150
Sauce, Spinach Coconut Lu'au—159
Sauce, Tailgate Teri—111
Sauteed Opakapaka with Spinach Coconut Lu'au Sauce—159
sauté—86, 146, 159, 166
scallops—14, 43, 69, 89, 105, 128, 182
Schiess, Walter—67
sea bass—14, 105
seafood—6, 7, 8, 14, 17, 19, 25, 27, 28, 34, 36, 37, 41, 43, 50, 53, 59, 60, 69, 72, 77, 86, 89, 101, 105, 128, 179, 181, 182, 183, 184, 186, 187, 189, 190, 191, 195
Seared Nihoa Opah—164
searing—115
seasoning salt—115

seaweed—24, 25, 27, 28, 30, 33, 34, 37, 47, 48, 53, 166, 201
Sesame Ginger Snap Peas—83
sesame seeds—28, 48, 55, 83, 95, 169
shallots—8, 21, 59, 71, 175
Sheen, Charlie—85
Sheldrake, Tommy Jean—148
shellfish—178
sherbet—214
sherry—60, 62, 70, 77, 80, 84, 88, 96, 122, 141, 147, 150, 158, 189
shiitake mushrooms—8, 43, 147, 150, 164, 201
shiso (beefsteak plant)—4
short ribs—123
shoyu—194
shoyu chicken—7
Shrimp Curry with Coconut Milk and Sugar Snap Peas—179
shrimp—6, 8, 17, 43, 50, 53, 86, 101, 178, 179, 181, 184, 186, 187, 190
Sichuan peppercorns—65
Simmer Shoyu Sugar Butterfish with Vegetables—198
slaw—45
Smoked Shrimp with Mango Salsa—190
snappers—105
soba—69
sodium—vii
somen—33
soup—11, 13, 14, 15, 19
sorbet, mango guava—212
soy sauce—x, 17
Spicy Braised Chicken with Ginger—65
Spinach Coconut Lu'au Sauce—159
spinach—8, 19, 46, 50, 69, 86, 118, 159
squash—119, 142
squid—195
Stant, David (Kawika)—199, 206
Stant, Elena—206
Stant, Lorie—203
star anise—18, 65
star fruit—45
steam fish fillets—154
Steamed Chicken with Lup Cheong—140
steaming—117, 139
stir fry—60, 77, 78, 88, 122, 181, 189
Stir-Fried Chicken or Beef Fajitas—148
Stir-Fried Curried Scallops—89
Stir-Fried Lobster and Tomatoes with Black Beans—189
Stir-Fried U-10 Shrimps and Fresh Asparagus—181
stock—21
Straight Hawaiian-Style 'Inamona Poke—27
strawberries—45, 207
Stuffed 'Ahi with Hana Butter and Papaya Coulis—169
stuffing—151
Sugar Peas, Please, vignette—47
sugar cane—17
sugar snap peas—47, 83, 122, 179
Summer 'Ahi Tartare—4

summer soup—x
sumo—199
Sun Bear Produce—47
Sunset Beach—127
Susser, Allen—85
Sweet Potato Casserole—129
sweet & sour sauce—171
sweet potato—14, 41, 129, 151
Sweet-Bread Variations for the Grill—109
sweet-bread—146
Swift, John and Vicki—146
swordfish (shutome)—104, 169
Swordfish, Mango and Garlic Bread Kebabs—104

Tailgate Annie Barbecue Leg of Lamb—108
Tailgate Mochi Mochi Chicken—10
Tailgate Teri Sauce—111
Tailgate Teri Steaks—99
tako (octopus)—28, 36
Tako Poke—36
tako tips, cooking tips—36
taro leaves—118, 123, 159
taro—19, 41, 201
tarragon—21
tartare—4, 25, 85
Teflon—76
teriyaki—155, 195
teriyaki sauce—99
Teriyaki Squid Tokyo Style—195
the other secret ingredient (orange juice), cooking tip—98
They Licked the Bowls, vignette—11
thick soy—77
Three-Fruit Sherbet—214
ti leaves—145, 161
toasting coconut, cooking tip—207
toasting macadamia nuts, cooking tip—3
toasting sesame seeds, cooking tip—55
Tabasco—183
tofu—vii, 81, 83, 198, 200, 201
Tokyo—163
Tomato Crab—191
tomatoes—36, 51, 53, 55, 59, 110, 126, 171, 184, 189, 191
Tony Luke's—103
Tony Roma—102
tortilla chips—33
tortillas—33, 110
Tropical Marmalade—20
Tropical Salsa—167
trout—117
Tsukiji Fish Market, Tokyo—154, 163, 183, 194, 202
Tsukiji Fish Market, vignette—163
tuna (aku, tombo)—169
turkey—81
TV cooking show—85, 161

Udon (thick noodles)—201
uku (grey snapper)—105, 172
Upcountry Sausage "Stuff It" Chicken—151
upcountry Maui—151

Vanilla sauce—209
vegetables—122, 148, 155, 171, 184, 191, 196, 198, 201
vegetarians—vii
vignettes, Crawfish Country—183
   Decade of the Chef—85
   Deglazing Grace—67
   Emu vs. Imu—145
   500 'Ahi—31
   Mom's Story: 'He Never Looked Back'—215
   My Friend Must Wait—127
   Philly Steak Sand With—103
   Sam in Japan—199
   Sugar Peas, Please—47
   They Licked the Bowls—11
   Tsukiji Fish Market—163

Waldorf-Astoria—209
walnuts—211
water chestnuts—50
watercress—198, 201
watermelon farm in Kunia, O'ahu—40
wawae'iole (seaweed)—30
Weeber, Larry—199
weke'ula (red goatfish)—163
whiskey—132
Why Not? Breadfruit, Sweet Potato and Taro Salad with Crabmeat—41
wine—21, 43, 69, 144, 172, 173, 175, 182, 184
wing beans—122
Wings of Wings Miso Shoyu Chicken—7
Wok Barbecue Shrimp with Pepper-Papaya-Pineapple Chutney—6

Wok Pork, Pineapple Barbecue Sauce and Lychees—84
Wok Spicy Tofu—81
Wok Stir-Fried Chicken with Sweet Peppers and Onions—78
Wok Stir-Fried Ono and Hawaiian Hot Peppers—88
Wok the Chicken with Eggplant & Hot Peppers—80
Wok-Fried Lobster with Thick Soy—77
wok—6, 7, 76, 77, 78, 80, 81, 84, 88
won bok (Napa cabbage)—201
Wong, Raymond—ii
Worcestershire sauce—107
"Wow the Neighbors" Seafood Salad

Yamato (Kalima, George)—199, 202
Yellowfin Tuna with Lime-Shoyu Marinade—96
yogurt—45, 217

Zucchini—69, 16

Hawaiiana Props

'opihi (edible limpet)—35
bowl (kamani wood)—52
bowls (milo wood)—42
drum (ipu heke, gourd drum)—124
fishnet—49
ipu heke (gourd drum)—124
kapa (tapa)—52
koa wood plate—12
kupe'e (Nerita polita, edible shellfish)—4
lauhala (pandanus) mat—12

lei ,'a'ali'i (Dodonaea)—44
lei hulu (feather lei)—121
lei pupu Ni'ihau—90
lei wili ('a'ali'i, bozu, kangaroo paws, likolehua, palapalai fern)—97
lei wili—79
lei'akulikuli (pink, rose & orange ice plant flowers)—124
lei, pansies—112
lei, red feather (52)
lei, red wiliwili seed—61
lei, seed (kukui, plumeria & wiliwili)—149
lei, seed (Manila palm & false wiliwili)—188
luhe'e (octopus lure)—29
naupaka (native shrub)—29
palaka (block-print cloth)—106
paniolo (cowboy) spurs, ropes, etc.—106
petroglyphs—9
poho kukui (kukui lamp)—26

Artists' Credits

Aguiar, David—(lei) 188, (seed lei) 61
Allen, Chris—(koa chopsticks) 90
Bryan, Jennifer & Corky—(kapa/tapa) 52
Bustu, Jimmy—(koa ukulele) 100
Choy, Moana Wai Lin—(lei hulu) 121
De Luz, Dan—(koa butter dish) 12, (avacado wood bowl & luhe'e/octopus lure) 29, (milo wood bowl) 35, (bowl) 176
Dunn, Kelly—(Norfolk pine wood platter) 61
Enomoto, Edmund—(ceramic bowl) 180, 185, 188

Hamakua Clay Co.—(ti-leaf plate) 116
Hirata, Paul—(pineapple salt & pepper shakers) 12
Hoe, Calvin—(ipu) 124
Joyce, Felix—(throw net) 49
Key, James—(seed lei) 149
Lappala, Dan—(koa tongs) 138
Lawless, Sara—(ki'i scuptures) 73
Locals Only—(vintage fabrics) 100
Louis the Fisher—(jade turtle pendant) 82
Lum, Keali'i T.M.—(ipu heke) 124
McDonald, Marie—(lei) 44, 97, 112, 124
Miyano, Babs—(glass platters) 68
Pali, Belinda—(kupe'e necklace) 4
Pico, Tom—(chief's food bowl) 52
Rivera, Joe—(etched-glass lantern) 68, (fish etched-glass bricks) 116
Rosato, Amy—(lei wili) 79, (ti-leaf lei) 116
Sater, Sandy—(laua'e/ceramic platter) 42
Tanabe, Carol—(feather lei) 52
Thurlby, Miles—(raku bowls) 157
Wagner, Gary—(turtle petroglyph plate) 9, (petroglyph etched-blass bowl & candleholders) 44
Warner, Julie—(ceramic platter) 121, (raku sushi plate) 157
Weeks, Junko—(petroglyph-print silk scarf) 79
White, Craig—(poho kukui /kukui lamps & stone bowls) 26, (carved stone bowl) 160
Wolfe, Rochelle—(hand-dyed sarong) 68, 130, (hand-dyed fabric) 168

SAM'S LAST WORDS

I would like to acknowledge the dream team that worked on this book — writer Catherine Enomoto; designers Leo Gonzalez and Randall Chun; photographer Douglas Peebles; food stylist Faith Ogawa; nutritionist Joannie Dobbs; and project coordinator Jane Hopkins; and pressed into service during crunch time — Ui and Steven Goldsberry and Raymond Wong.

I would also like to acknowledge publisher Bennett Hymer; his assistants Galyn Wong, Betsy Kubota, Eve Brant, and marketing specialist Kei Furukawa; my secretary Aileen Steele for wearing 20 different hats; my bookkeeper Joann Ewaliko for always making me land on my feet; my chefs Mike Longworth, Marcus Aickin and Derek Yee in Honolulu and Paul Muranaka in Kona; my Honolulu partner James Lee for being supportive in allowing us to do fun projects; and the countless people who made this book a reality.